Social Justice:

Politics, Technology and Culture for a Better World

# Social Justice: Politics, Technology and Culture for a Better World

*edited by*

Susan Magarey

Wakefield Press

Wakefield Press
Box 2266
Kent Town
South Australia 5071

First published 1998

Design and typesetting by Michael Deves, Adelaide
Printed and bound by Hyde Park Press, Adelaide

ISBN 1 86254 477 8

# Contents

*Susan Magarey*

# Introduction

Popular conceptions of university researchers depict an egghead in an ivory tower, remote from the concerns of ordinary people and their worlds, carrying out esoteric and useless work at the tax-payers' expense. Perhaps it is such conceptions that drive current government policies relating to university research, and in particular, research in the humanities and social sciences. The end of the twentieth century is not a good time for the humanities and social sciences in Australian universities. Student numbers are falling; government funding is being cut; universities are having to sack staff; in some cases whole departments— particularly in the humanities and social sciences—are being closed down. And funding to support research, especially in the humanities and social sciences, is shrinking in real terms.

In 1998 the Academy of the Humanities in Australia produced a three-volume report entitled *Knowing Ourselves and Others: The Humanities in Australia into the 21st Century*. This report defended the intrinsic importance of research in the humanities to our national life. It also produced a cogent response to—and refusal of—such isolated, research-nerd representations. (The Academy of the Social Sciences produced a parallel report some months later in the same year.) In relation to the intrinsic centrality of such research, the Humanities Report argued that

> It constantly generates new knowledge about the human condition and human experience. It widens horizons, deepens sensibilities, sharpens awareness. It regularly reinterprets past knowledge in the light of new devel-opments in understanding. A great deal of it is extensively committed to

Associate Professor Susan Magarey, Director of the Adelaide Research Centre for Humanities and Social Sciences, Director of the Research Centre for Women's Studies and founding Editor of *Australian Feminist Studies*, an international journal, is author of the prize-winning study, *Unbridling the tongues of women: a biography of Catherine Helen Spence* (Hale & Iremonger) 1985; co-editor of *Debutante Nation: Feminism contests the 1890s* (Allen & Unwin) 1993 and of *Women in Restructuring Australia: Work and Welfare* (Allen & Unwin) 1995.

> transmitting the great storehouses of accumulated knowledge to new
> generations. It contributes crucially to the preservation of common standards
> of citizenship, to the strengths of inherited cultures, and to the viability of
> attested values through all the vicissitudes of changing social, cultural and
> economic circumstances. It provides enrichment of the mind through the
> study of what men and women of many creeds and cultures have created
> down the centuries.[1]

Research in the humanities, and the social sciences, constitutes, the Report
maintains, 'a great cultural resource'. It is a 'medium for social criticism'; it is a
vehicle for exploring and debating 'crucial social and cultural values'; it is a
mechanism for 'fathoming the social phenomena within which we live'.[2]

But the Report does not rely on this resounding justification alone. Its compilers
recognise that at the end of the twentieth century we are once again in an over-
whelmingly utilitarian era. Yet, it maintains, it is easy to demonstrate the usefulness of humanities research. It answers our need to know about all manner of
issues associated with the European heritage of the greater part of our population.

> These range from such matters as those key governmental concepts,
> 'Democracy', 'Bureaucracy', 'Citizenship', 'Parliamentary Government', 'Civil
> Order', 'the Rule of Law', through a host of other matters, and not least the
> languages of Europe itself, English most particularly, to, for some amongst us,
> such highly personal questions as, for example, how it was that the Holocaust
> could ever have happened, or why it was that in the former Yugoslavia there
> should lately have been so brutal a civil war.[3]

Can one even begin to imagine the possibility of a National Convention on the
Australian Constitution, without information, debate and understandings about
such basic matters being widespread?

Humanities research answers our needs to know about our own country, about
Aboriginal history and culture, and about our neighbours, especially those in Asia.
It can help to address acute problems of literacy in some sections of the Australian
population. It provides practitioners and commentators who can speak 'knowl-
edgeably and illuminatingly' to a widespread and growing interest in the Arts.
Further, since Australia is geographically ideally-placed, as an English-speaking
nation in the Asia-Pacific region, to export particular educational commodities to
the region, Australia's research in the humanities could readily provide 'English-
language capabilities and its knowledge of Western Humanities disciplines' to a
region where, as throughout the world, English will become the international language of the twenty-first century.[4]

Scholars in the humanities are increasingly participating in the work of public
history, business ethics, medical ethics, tourism, town planning and questions
around heritage, and humanities research provides knowledge and competency
which informs a great deal of the competencies and skills of those working in the
mushrooming communications industries.[5] Research in the humanities, and in

the social sciences, is, then, vital to Australia's economic, as well as our social and political well-being and vitality.

The articles collected here support such arguments. But they take them further, too. For these articles also foreground the essentially political nature of the arguments that they develop. To say this is not to suggest that these articles are concerned with matters that should or could be exclusively the subject of debate in our parliaments, or among the formulators of public policy in our bureaucracies. Rather, such a claim mobilises a broader conception of 'the political' as anything concerned with differences of power between people—as individuals, groups, races, sexes, nations.

Such a conception of power enables us to explore, with Philip Butterss, the ways in which the power of particular versions of masculinity in Australian films—the hegemonic masculinity which operates to maintain men's dominant position in the culture—may have been more complex and divided in the past than recollection of only tough, macho, bushrangers would allow. More recently, too, as Butterss outlines, Australian films have called into question such images of a monocultural nation, and associated conceptions of a single, unified, masculinity. Such a conception of power allows us to pursue, with Deane Fergie, an analysis of the ways in which 'the Outback' in Australia has been created, and re-created, in popular media representations, to accord with notions formed in the metropolises rather than in those regions held to be the locations of the Outback, an analysis which highlights the differences in power—over even the ways in which their own lives and environments are imaged—between those who live in the cities and those who live in rural Australia. Such a conception of power enables us to follow Andrew Watson's examination of the diplomatic and trading relations between Australia and China, and the ways in which these have shifted in response to imperatives which are also as political, in the narrower sense, as they are economic and strategic.

Furthermore, these articles show a strong commitment to a democratic sharing of power—to social justice. Graeme Hugo's article is the clearest illustration of this point. One of the principal imperatives for the research under way in the National Key Centre for Geographical Information Systems (GIS), he states, is to re-instate people at the heart of the process of planning. This could be seen as an ironic claim, since the geographical information systems that he describes depend on highly sophisticated, computerised, information and communications technology. Yet Hugo demonstrates how such technology can be mobilised to improve the ways in which social planners reach decisions about a host of policy matters, ranging from the provision of health and transport services to the elderly, through establishing optimal locations of new educational facilities for a changing population, and assessing the insurance risk for all of the buildings in Adelaide, to quicker and better informed responses to bushfire. These information systems can be used to answer questions as local as the sources of support for the South

Australian National Football League (the Adelaide Crows) and as international as planning the distribution of new secondary schools throughout Indonesia. They can empower communities: Hugo's prime example is the website of the Friends of the Earth in Britain which uses geographical information systems to show, for instance, the levels of pollution in any area. People can click onto their home area, and if they discover that they are living with high levels of pollution, they then have sound information around which to organise protests or lobbying groups to have the pollution reduced. Central to all such projects, as Hugo reaffirms in his conclusion, is a commitment to arresting and reversing the manifest growing inequality in Australian society.

A similar commitment to sharing power more equally can be discerned in Butterss' demonstration of ways in which some films have shown increasing recognition that, despite a hegemonic masculinity, there are other ways of being a man in Australia today; 'subordinated masculinities such as those lived by homosexual men, or masculinities marginalised from mainstream power by race or class'. It is there, too, in Fergie's analysis of the need for the people of the mythical Outback—black and white, both—to speak for and about themselves, instead of being spoken for and about by city folk who do not know what they are talking about—a need at the centre of national political debate over competing rights to land in the late 1990s. Similar commitment surfaces, Watson shows, in Australia's concern with China's policies concerning human rights, though, as he notes as well, other countries could, and have, expressed concern about Australia's own policies concerning human rights. And in Penny Boumelha's discussion of the place of culture in an age of information, which begins this volume, there is an uncompromising statement of commitment to the investigation of, and contribution to, a society's significant social, moral and environmental issues.

In an age of information, she points out—particularly an age dominated by the economic utilitarianism addressed by *Knowing Ourselves and Others*—knowledge is predominantly discussed as a commodity with an identifiable market value. But such representation is just as much a metaphor as other representations of the pursuit of knowledge—as colonial exploration and heroic discovery, for instance, or as ingenious invention and manufacture, or even as a boom in the building industry, with foundations being laid and frameworks constructed. One metaphor which Boumelha favours is that appearing in a description of the research culture in the humanities in terms of biodiversity and ecosystem, a balanced and interdependent environment. 'The coming to dominance of an ecological paradigm of knowledge generation would', she observes, 'present a quite different picture from that of the impersonal workings of the market'. For her central concern is with what is distinctive, and intrinsically important, about research in the humanities, a concern over which she joins hands with the authors of the review of the humanities throughout Australia.

In her argument, it is 'a preoccupation with culture'. By this, she does not mean 'culture' in the sense of a term of approbation, as when we praise someone for being cultured. Nor does she mean the opposite of nature, for instance, or barbarism. She is not using the term to refer, narrowly, to the performing arts and literature. And she is not implying a single, or consensual, idea of culture which as she notes, might be highly multicultural. Rather, as she says:

> Culture as it focuses research in the humanities and social sciences is what makes a society—any society—a society: the set of practices, values and meanings by which it constructs itself as a society, and within which individuals come to understand their relation to society. Culture, in brief, is what makes life in society meaningful.

The culture, the meanings, manifest in the articles in this volume give heart to those who would, amid the present erosion of all but the utilitarian with its market value, declare 'the death of the university'. Despite their very different objects and means of analysis, all of these articles evince a profound allegiance to the preservation and extension of human rights—to social justice.

The chapters in this book began life as public lectures presented to the Adelaide community to launch a new initiative of the University of Adelaide. This is the establishment of the Adelaide Research Centre for Humanities and Social Sciences (ARCHSS), which aims—among other things—to foster and promote community access to research under way in the humanities and social sciences, and appreciation of the value of that research to everyone. We would like to express our gratitude to F.H. Faulding for funding for these lectures, and to Radio 5UV for recording them and broadcasting them. I would like to thank Mary Lyons for all her work in organising those lectures, Greta Larsen for all her work in preparing them for publication, and Peter Murdoch for his help with the visuals.

## Notes

1 *Knowing Ourselves and Others. The Humanities in Australia into the 21st Century*, 3 vols, Prepared by a Reference Group for the Australian Academy of the Humanities (Australian Government Publishing Services), Canberra, April 1998, vol. 1, p. 6
2 Ibid.
3 *Knowing Ourselves*, vol. 1, p. 7.
4 *Knowing Ourselves*, vol. 1, pp. 7-8.
5 *Knowing Ourselves*, vol. 1, p. 8.

*Penny Boumelha*

# Culture in the Age of Information: Knowledge and Research in the Humanities and Social Sciences

'Research! A mere excuse for idleness; it has never achieved and will never achieve any results of the slightest value.'[1] Such, at least, was the view of the nineteenth-century Oxford academic Benjamin Jowet. To say the least of it, matters have changed rather fundamentally in tertiary education since Jowet, and research is now generally considered to be among the most important and the most prestigious aspects of university activity. Professionalised and prioritised, quantified and quality audited, centrally planned and strategically managed, research is now supposed to occupy on average about a third of the working time of every academic. The name 'research' covers the whole spectrum from basic, so-called 'curiosity-driven' research, impelled primarily by the desire of the researcher to push an unasked question, an important issue or a new hypothesis as far as it will go, to close commercial cooperation on pressing industrial or technological needs with research and development in private companies. Not only is it on occasion closely allied with big business, but in a number of respects it *is* big business, attracting, generating and spending large amounts of money—university expenditure on research was about $2 billion per annum in 1994 and 1995[2]—and employing a whole workforce of academic, technical, managerial, administrative and other support staff.

To those scholars in the humanities and social sciences who began their research careers hunched for hours at a time over their accumulation of books and documents in the lovingly-fostered silence and solitude of a major research

Penny Boumelha, Jury Professor of English Language and Literature; Head of the Division of Humanities and Social Sciences; and Dean of Arts, is the author of *Thomas Hardy and Women: Sexual Ideology and Narrative Form* (Harvester Press, UK; Barnes and Noble, USA) 1982, reprinted 1984; paperback (Wisconsin University Press) 1984; and *Charlotte Bronte* (Harvester Wheatsheaf, UK; Indiana University Press, USA) 1990.

library, this world of intellectual property, patents, performance indicators and input-output relativities can be bewildering and alienating. There is no doubt that research has changed: its nature, its private and social benefits, its relationship to teaching, have all been reconceptualised in recent years. Most notably and often excitingly, the practices of research have in many instances been transformed by communications and information technology. E-mail and the internet, for example, have made quick and regular communication between research groups, collaborators and even total strangers extraordinarily easy, and saved a great deal of time and money that might once have spent on travel ( a particular bonus for scholars in Australia). Electronic access to the on-line catalogues of great libraries around the world, easily accessible databases, document delivery services, electronic journals, video-conferenced seminars, have greatly speeded up—and some would say depersonalised—the basic processes of humanities and social sciences research: access to materials, accumulation of data, publication. It is now perfectly possible to engage in genuinely collaborative work with a fellow researcher on the other side of the world without ever actually meeting them. In research as in other sectors of the economy, information has significantly displaced the primacy of the major economic factors of labour, plant and capital.[3]

This sounds like a wonderful scenario, and in many ways it certainly is. It is not without its problems and its dangers, however. One of them, for those of us in the humanities and social sciences, is that, paradoxical as it might seem, access to our fundamental research data is to a degree threatened by the demand upon library budgets which are now expected to cover the full range of advanced electronic services as well as the printed books and journals that have traditionally been their responsibility. Since the continuation of free access to electronic data-bases is uncertain, this threat becomes even more acute.[4] Certainly there are disciplines in which the most urgent research need is access to an article published last week on the other side of the world; but there are also others in which the ability to handle directly a seventeenth century pamphlet is an absolute fundamental. Archival researchers deal constantly and of necessity with materials which may well never be reproduced in any technological medium, and the fear that the basic materials of research will become inaccessible to them is only partially offset by the ease of e-mail communication with a fellow specialist elsewhere.

Another problem—by no means peculiar to the humanities and social sciences—is that the very accessibility of information can sometimes become burdensome. The current high estimation of information—in the sense of facts, data—for its own sake tends to mean that scholars and writers feel obliged to follow up every reference of conceivable relevance and then to include it, however tangential its relation to the project in hand. I am sure I am not the only reader who thinks that a book of 700 pages is not necessarily superior to a book of 250 pages; I have certainly read far too many works of scholarship in recent years that provide twenty examples to support an argument where two would do, and far too many biographies in which every tiny piece of information is included simply because it is possible to find it. I sometimes wonder whether the task of writing a thesis is on the verge of becoming impossible for postgraduates in the humanities and social sciences; the encyclopaedic tendency to chase up every title, read every reference and then include it *because* you have read it is always a trap for new players, and the accessibility of ever-expanding fields of information to a highly computer literate generation does nothing to arrest that tendency. A little earlier, I identified the accumulation of materials and publication as two areas eased by new technologies. What they have not necessarily helped is the important part of the activity that makes research research: the unpredictable bit in the middle— thinking. The explosion in the volume of material to be consulted does not necessarily simplify the tasks of interpretation, argument and analysis, and it may well be that a conceptual transformation akin to the technological revolution will be needed if research practices are to remain sustainable.[5]

Such problems may well be solved by higher levels of research policy co-ordination or by further technological advances, and it is undeniable that developments in communications technology in particular have made some aspects of research across the entire range of university disciplines quicker, easier and often cheaper. The already major impact of information technologies has been greatly increased, however, by the phenomenon often known as 'globalisation.' Like many words of urgent contemporary relevance, this one still has rather fluid and evolving meanings for the moment. It will probably be enough for my purposes here if we take it to identify the way in which the telescoping of time and space has *delocalised* so much of experience and communication, making them present everywhere and nowhere at the same time. Distance, time differences, even cultural differences, have been reduced to insignificance in the world of the new technologies. Globalisation is a phenomenon of the economy, of trade, of culture and of communication. Australia's geographical isolation means that it has been—and will be—particularly affected by globalisation. The power of barriers of time and space is already diminished, and the measures (such as tariff regulations) that have in the past served to reinforce economic frontiers are becoming increasingly unworkable as free market capitalism establishes itself as the language of the global economy.[6]

In this context, information technology has offered significant infrastructural support to the recent recasting of universities as business corporations engaged in what is known as the 'knowledge industry': that is, the provision of information, data and expertise on a commercial basis outside the traditional parameters of teaching and research. Certainly Bill Gates is in no doubt about the connection between information technology and commercialisation: his idea of the network, he writes, is as 'the ultimate market ... It will be where we social animals will sell, trade, invest, haggle, pick stuff up, argue, meet new people and hang out. When you hear the phrase "information highway," rather than seeing a road, imagine a marketplace or an exchange.'[7] The knowledge industry offers a new mission which universities, in Australia as elsewhere, have embraced with varying degrees of enthusiasm. Since universities are places whose existence is primarily justified by the concentration of knowledge and information to be found there, they might hope to become key players in such an industry, using their own entrepreneurial efforts to supplement declining recurrent government funding by orienting their teaching and research more clearly towards market needs.

It is a prospect, though, that troubles many academics, for whom the free circulation of knowledge and research findings is at once an aim and a tool of their most valued activities. Perhaps I am naive in suggesting that most researchers carry out research in order to make their results known and not in order to own them. In any case, for many (though not all) of the disciplines of the humanities and social sciences, there is considerable improbability in the idea that their research will have significant market value. The most abiding images of research, I suppose, are the major breakthroughs, discoveries or inventions capable of making an immediately discernible difference to the world. In some spectacular instances, both the commercial value and the social benefits are obvious and tangible. It has to be said that rather little research in the humanities and social sciences is of that kind; certainly there is valuable and important applied research—most particularly, perhaps, in disciplines such as psychology and geography—but it is probably as well to admit from the outset that it is unlikely to be in a Faculty of Arts that an AIDS vaccine will be developed, a disease-resistant strain of a vital agricultural crop genetically engineered, or a major advance in passenger aircraft safety proposed. But I shall want to go on, a little later, to propose that academic work in the humanities and social sciences offers rewards—personal and social—much like those of any basic research: unpredictable, incalculable and diffuse in their contribution to knowledge.

Of course, some still operative definitions of knowledge would appear in any case to exclude much of what goes on in the social sciences and, especially, the humanities. This definition is Harry Maddox's:

> If we know something we should be able to justify it and explain why it is true, cite evidence for it and show how it can be verified. Even when a belief is true it is still not knowledge unless the believer can substantiate it and show why it is true.[8]

Such an argument works well enough for experimental disciplines, for example, where verification and refutation can be achieved by repetition of experiment and analysis of methodology. It has very little to do with much academic work in the humanities and social sciences, though; it is not in any real sense possible to *disprove* another scholar's contention that colour imagery in Wordsworth, say, is the key to understanding Romanticism (though it is certainly possible to argue a different or contradictory view), nor to *verify* by empirical means a theory of the construction of gendered subjectivities in patriarchal societies. One of the reasons why much research in the humanities and social sciences fits so uncomfortably into many current practices and measures is that it is often less about discovery, invention, or even proof, than about *persuasion.* Of course, all research is to some degree dependent for its recognition and impact on the judicious assessment of other scholars and specialists, who will reproduce its methodology, examine its evidence or challenge its conclusions. Without the rigorous testing provided by others, no researcher could feel entirely satisfied by their own results. But more than most, research in the humanities and social sciences can only be endorsed by its ability to convince others of its cogency, its probability, its explanatory power, or its coherence. Such qualities can only be tested by open, vigorous debate and usually not, for example, by the repetition of a series of experiments. For these reasons it is not easily assimilated into the ideology of privatisation and commercialisation, patents and intellectual property, that currently drives so much of the research sector. Such research is only active, in a way only *exists,* if it is in open circulation with others who are concerned with the same issues. It simply makes no sense to have intellectual property rights over a proposed textual emendation to Act IV of *King Lear* when only its adoption by others will confirm its significance.

I am aware that to say 'knowledge is not an object to be bought and sold' has the ring of emotional rhetoric, but there is also a sense in which it is the literal truth. As a look at the scholarly apparatus of footnotes and references in any academic publication will confirm, ideas almost never—perhaps absolutely never—belong to an individual, however original, gifted or iconoclastic. Sometimes 'new' ideas are the result of teamwork or collaboration, often they are developments from ideas proposed by others, even more often their very novelty consists of new interpretations, connections or syntheses of ideas already at large in the culture. Even if we shift attention from ownership to exchange, the property concept still does not translate well to the field of knowledge, as Peter Sheldrake has pointed out:

> the concept of property implies that an individual has right to something, and can 'alienate' that right to another: I own a car, and then, when I sell it, I no longer have any right of property in that vehicle. Try to use that model with knowledge: I have developed some new ideas, and then I sell them to another, but I still have the ideas—I can't alienate them in the same way that I disposed of the car.[9]

I should not wish for a moment to deny the reality and far-reaching importance of the information industry in advanced industrialised economies. I believe, too, that universities have an obligation to be responsible and accountable in their use of public money, that they are right to make use of the legal and commercial protection offered to innovation by patents and intellectual property rights, and that it is essential to be commercially alert in order to provide as much unfettered funding as possible to maintain the range and quality of their activities. Nevertheless, it is important, in my view, to recognise that knowledge as a commodity is in the end a *metaphor* which derives its current dominance in the research culture from its perhaps momentary coalescence with economic and technological developments. It is, of course, not a new metaphor. In his great defence of free speech, *Areopagitica,* the poet Milton urged in 1644 that:

> Truth and understanding are not such wares as to be monopolized and traded
> in by tickets, and statutes, and standards. We must not think to make a staple
> commodity of all the knowledge in the land, to mark and license it like our
> broadcloth and our woolpacks.[10]

The pursuit of new knowledge has been variously figured at different times and in different contexts: as colonial exploration and heroic discovery, the pushing back of frontiers and the mapping of the *terra nullius* of ideas; as ingenious invention and manufacture; as the evolution of a cumulative body of knowledge through epistemic natural selection; even as a boom in the building industry, with the laying of foundations and the construction of frameworks.[11] Each of these metaphors—and of course the many more I might have cited—has some degree of correlation with historical processes or social ideologies of progress. The 'supermarket of ideas'[12] and the play of market forces are no less marked by the prevailing discourses of their time. To say that something is a metaphor is by no means to dismiss its usefulness or its importance (as a Professor of English Language and Literature, I could hardly think so!). Language without some kind of figurative dimension is in any case virtually unimaginable. Nevertheless, metaphor is in itself neither fact nor argument, and it is possible to overlook the emergence of new paradigms, new understandings, if its figurative quality too often goes unnoticed. I have already observed, for example, that the research culture is coming to be described here and there (for example, in a recent report on research funding in the Humanities)[13] in terms of biodiversity and ecosystem, a balanced and interdependent environment. The coming to dominance of an ecological paradigm of knowledge generation would present a quite different picture from that of the impersonal workings of the market.

I should like to turn now from this rather general account of current trends in research to a closer look at how the humanities and social sciences fit within it. Research in these areas varies greatly in its concerns and practices across and within individual disciplines, and I do not propose to try to negotiate the variations across the continuum that runs from the extremes of, say, physical geography or experimental psychology at one end to editing a manuscript in Old French at the other. I should probably acknowledge to my colleagues in the social science disciplines that my own background in literary studies may give what follows something of a humanities bias. I do not think it is a misrepresentation of any discipline in the humanities and social sciences, though, to say that they broadly share a preoccupation with culture. Culture in this sense is not a term of approbation—as when we praise someone for being cultured—and implies no polarity with any possible opposite, such as nature or barbarism. Nor do I mean it as another term for the performing arts and literature. Culture as it focuses research in the humanities and social sciences is what makes a society—*any* society—a society: the set of practices, values and meanings by which it constructs itself as a society, and within which individuals come to understand their relation to society. Culture, in brief, is what makes life in society meaningful.[14] I should make clear that this does not imply a single or consensual idea of culture, which might, for example, be highly multicultural. Indeed, one of the great pleasures in working in these disciplines is what Jonathan Culler has called the 'instruction in otherness' they provide, their vivid and palpable evidence of differences in cultures, values and assumptions.[15]

For quite some time there was perceived to be an inherent opposition between the sciences and the disciplines concerned with culture. That perception rests upon the construction of a set of false oppositions between facts and intuitions, the objective and the subjective, the analytic and the empathetic. That particular perception has passed away, I think, for a variety of reasons, including the blurring of boundaries; professors of physics now speak about metaphysics and theology, discourse analysts now bring their skills to bear on scientific writing. Tensions still persist, of course, and especially in the context of competitive funding for research. A clear community of interest has arisen, though, from the shared plight of much of the basic (as I said, 'curiosity-driven') research absolutely central to scientific advance and much research in the humanities and social sciences. Both are devalued and endangered by the current dominance of the idea that research must be of demonstrable and specific utility if it is to be supported. There are obvious reasons why it is perfectly appropriate for any government to identify research priorities linked to economic objectives and industrial development. Equally, non-government research funding sources are justified in identifying their own areas of need and consequent priority for support. The cumulative effect of the utilitarian turn, though, poses very significant difficulties for the continuing presence of research premised upon unpredictability of outcomes and diffuseness of effect. If the marketability of a research project figures too predominantly in the list of factors for grant success, for example, it will change the balance and conception of research activity across large areas of academic endeavour in ways that may not prove beneficial in any long-term perspective.

It is far too easy simply to moan about being undervalued, underfunded and under scrutiny, in my view, and the intellectual debilitation of continuous complaint is only the more likely to ensure failure. There are productive and inventive responses within a number of disciplines to the entrepreneurialist pressures of the moment. Ken Ruthven has pointed out that the developing of public history out of history, heritage management out of archaeology, applied ethics out of philosophy, and cultural policy studies out of cultural studies all demonstrate the capacity of even the most resolutely non utilitarian of disciplines to adapt positively and productively to their environment.[16] In the end, though, it is not in such 'soft instrumentalism', to use Simon Marginson's term,[17] that the benefits and significance of research in the humanities and social sciences must be demonstrated. I shall attend very little to such benefits in the discussion that follows about those aspects of our research activity which make a clearly perceptible contribution to the public good; but I do not want any of my colleagues in, say, demography or labour research to imagine that this means I have forgotten them. It is simply that the real case that needs to be made, publicly and repeatedly, is for the moment elsewhere.

Surveying the outlines of a range of not uncharacteristic projects in a hypothetical Arts Faculty—let us say, the elaboration of an ecological literary theory, an analysis of voting patterns in the election of 1987, a new interpretation of the historical significance of the Anglo-Saxon Chronicle, and a study of second language teaching techniques in Myanmar—any only slightly unfriendly observer might be forgiven for assuming that they have nothing to add to our knowledge and no contribution to make to social needs. I believe that this fairly common perception is based on a misrecognition, however, rather like that of characterising Mendel's founding studies in the discipline of genetics as looking at peas. The importance and value of any piece of research are not delimited just by its object of analysis. It is crucial also to look at its purpose, and therefore at the issues with which it is concerned. A recent article in the academic newspaper *Campus Review* confronted the utilitarian imperative head-on by arguing for the importance of what the writer called 'useless knowledge' in the humanities. I find myself rather more in sympathy with the subsequent correspondent to the paper who took exception to this characterisation: what could be more useful to a society, he asked, than investigation of and contribution to its significant social, moral and environmental issues?[18] In my view, no society can afford to settle only for knowing how to do things; questions touching upon the organisation and values of a society, the distribution of its resources, its understanding of and relation to its environments, and the role of its cultural texts in creating and transmitting ideologies and values will always have urgency and importance, whether they deal with the here and now or with other times and places. They are important *in themselves;* and they are also important in the framework of concepts and contexts they provide for research and debate on social, political and cultural issues.

Its focus on culture has in some respects proved to be a difficulty for some areas of research in the humanities and social sciences. Most people's direct experience will not be consciously shaped by, say, sub-atomic particle physics, and it is easy to concede the need for professional specialisation, specialist language and explanatory theories in an area of knowledge that seems by definition arcane. But when the material in question is experience shared by all or many—gender issues, say, or television soapies—the specialist can often encounter a kind of sceptical resentment. The interpretative frameworks and specialist language in place in that discipline may be perceived as somehow inherently pretentious, deliberately exclusive and demeaning of the experience and understanding of the so-called 'ordinary person'. But, important though it is to avoid cultivating difficulty for its own sake as a kind of credential of seriousness, I think it is necessary to defend specialisation. I must confess that I have never fully understood the anxiety, since all of us will have the experience of the amateur far more often and in many more contexts than that of the specialist. The existence of meteorologists, formidably equipped with databases and satellites, does not prevent my going outside and assessing whether the weather is good enough for a picnic; the hypotheses and analyses of even the most historiographically sophisticated of historians does not in the least prevent me from remembering the 1960s or speculating as to why student radicalism was so prevalent then and is so diminished now. In other words, the fact that an activity is susceptible to theorisation, interpretation or analysis does not transform its nature for those subjectively engaged in it without reference to such matters. As in every other branch of academic endeavour, the professional and specialist frameworks of research are what enable the necessary questions to be framed and the answers to be pursued. Research in any area demands rigorous, difficult work embodying reflection on its own practices and assumptions if it is to follow issues through to their fullest extent.[19]

The question of specialisation has become slightly complicated in the humanities and social sciences, though. Techniques, concerns and practices of research are never stable and fixed for very long, of course, but its fundamental aim remains the same: to make a contribution to knowledge by identifying new objects of enquiry and developing appropriate methodologies, techniques and skills to engage fruitfully with them. I have already referred to significant changes across the university sector, both under the pressure of economic and policy developments and in response to new technologies. Some of the most far-reaching changes in intellectual life in the humanities and social sciences, though, have not been what you might call externally imposed. Instead, they have been generated by shifts and pressures within the constitution of the disciplines themselves. Chief among them, in my view, is the great growth of a complex and sophisticated version of interdisciplinarity. Interdisciplinarity can be imagined as a kind of intellectual equivalent of the process of globalisation, in which frontiers cease to demarcate the limits of activity and local specificities are minimised. Its ultimate effects on how universities structure and organise their activities may be in their way as significant as those of the globalisation process.

The structure of most traditional universities reflects a particular understanding of academic disciplines: departments, each bearing the name of its discipline, represent both the content and the limits of particular modes of intellectual enquiry, and faculties represent a grouping by what might be called methodological affinity. Such a structure favours, and indeed presupposes, clear boundaries and identifiable contents. Relations between the disciplines function as a kind of wary neighbourliness: a cheery hello when you meet outside, and the occasional watchful eye to make sure they are not encroaching on your territory or dumping their rubbish in your backyard. In recent years, however, there has been an extra-ordinary disciplinary convergence which can make it difficult to determine from the name of a subject taught or the description of a research project where it 'belongs' in this traditional structure. Who teaches Freud, for instance? Psychology? Well yes, maybe, but it is just as likely to be Women's Studies or English or Politics or Anthropology or almost anywhere else. A department of English may as easily contain a specialist in legal discourse, a postcolonial theorist, a researcher in the sociology of the history of medicine and a film analyst as a Shakespeare scholar. Universities more recently established may contain no departments in the traditional disciplines of the humanities and social sciences, but feature instead schools of cultural studies or international studies and research centres on the history and theory of the body.

For some, I know, this permeability and dissolution of boundaries is a sinister prospect, threatening to merge carefully developed methodologies and painfully won analytical specificities into a kind of lumpy and indigestible intellectual porridge. For others, such disciplinary convergence has proved to be an intellec-tually exciting and academically fruitful experience, unlocking new areas of enquiry that somehow never quite emerged into view within the more rigidly structured disciplinary frameworks. Some disciplinary areas (such as my own) have taken to the new interdisciplinarity more readily than others. Terry Eagleton (also a literary scholar) is I think being only semi-facetious, for example, in the explanation he offers for this.

> In an age when traditional boundaries between intellectual disciplines are rapidly blurring, geography shares with literary studies the signal advantage of never having had much idea of what it was about in the first place. Just as literary studies covers everything from dactyls to death, geography spans everything from sand dunes to marriage rituals.[20]

This disciplinary convergence has been greatly enabled by the recognition of the shared status of much of the cultural and social theory that has reinvigorated research and teaching in the humanities and social sciences over the last two decades. A disciplinary colleague of mine, Ken Ruthven, has referred to such theory as the 'esperanto of the humanities'[21] and I am sure he intends it positively. I know, though, that many people regard Esperanto as a kind of impractical pipe-dream. So, I should like to pick up his linguistic metaphor slightly differently and suggest that intellectual conversation between the converging disciplines has been conducted in the academic equivalent of a pidgin: a theoretic language originally spoken by neither party, but evolved to enable exchange. (This large body of shared reference, incidentally, has also contributed significantly to the kind of information explosion to which I referred to earlier, and has its part to play in the 600-page monograph).

There is still at present a degree of tension between disciplinary purists and enthusiasts of interdisciplinarity, and it is not clear what the future holds in this respect. Both as a practising academic and as an administrator, I think it is important to do our best to provide a context that will allow both to flourish. I believe that the structures of departments and degrees that we currently have in place still provide the support that is needed to foster and sustain research and teaching within the disciplines as traditionally conceived; they are large enough, old enough and strong enough to take care of themselves quite effectively, and on the whole they do so extremely well. My own Faculty has attempted also to provide an element of corresponding structural support for the new interdisciplinarity. In teaching, we have done so by the introduction of a range of named degrees that allow us to focus on new objects of study across departmental boundaries. In research, a number of means have been used to foster new areas, and the chief among them is the new Adelaide Research Centre for Humanities and Social Sciences, providing a point of focus and support for the emerging, the innovative, the perhaps unorthodox. I hope it will continue to do so.

The Research Centre also has another important role, and that is to provide a place and a structure for the testing of our research and the communication of its results in the wider public context. Perhaps complacent, perhaps defensive and embattled, researchers in the humanities and social sciences have not always made enough effort to draw attention to their research, both in the academic and in the wider community. If the work of research itself is often hard, as I said earlier, there is no reason why the communication of its outcomes has to be so. I have argued that our research is focused on debate, contestation and persuasion, and it is important that we be prepared to take these beyond the conference platform and the walls of the university. Researchers in the humanities and social sciences have both the opportunity and the responsibility to take on the role of what is sometimes called the 'public intellectual', offering rigorous, informed and sometimes provocative commentary and analysis on major questions. I say it is a *responsibility* to do so because many of the significant issues preoccupying public debate in Australia are framed and conducted in concepts, values and arguments stemming from the humanities and social sciences. The other articles in this collection illustrate very clearly what I mean, addressing as they do concerns of gender relations, urban planning, citizenship, national identity, and Australia's relation to Asia. Racism and multi-culturalism, republicanism, environmentalism, the ethics of euthanasia, ways of tackling problems of domestic violence could easily form the basis of just such another collection. It would be quite wrong to settle for allowing academic research and public debate on such issues to run in parallel, unconnected and uncommunicative; productive interaction between them is essential. It is unimaginable that an article in an academic journal will ever bring its argument to the notice of as many people as a television debate or a newspaper column, and it is essential that we continue to look beyond the traditional scholarly outlets for the dissemination of our research results and professional expertise.

I am by no means arguing that we substitute a faculty full of television stars for the rigours of academic debate. The historian Ann Curthoys has pointed out the potential dangers in the role of the academic as public intellectual: it threatens to collapse the possibly incompatible 'need for public information' and the 'need to advance the frontiers of scholarship' into one another, she argues, and often obscures the questions of methodology and theory that are essential to both the conduct and the assessment of the research endeavour.[22] Most of all, she is concerned that the presentation of research results without the scholarly apparatus of footnotes and references will convey a false impression of research as a kind of smooth and harmonious narrative of consensually advancing knowledge. For Curthoys, it is essential that the *disputatiousness* of research be evident; it is not a tranquil scene of peaceful co-existence, but the site of the kinds of debate, contradiction, contention and counterclaim by which knowledge proceeds. This argument crystallises some important points. I would agree that the role of the academic in public debate is not to demonstrate what they know (or think they know), but to allow others to test and advance that knowledge. We must certainly not surrender rigour, difficulty or innovation in the interests of easy communicability; but nor must we fetishise inaccessibility as the currency of research. Above all, we must not allow ourselves to appear to be suggesting that final answers and incontestable analyses have settled any question. 'All human knowledge takes the form of interpretation,' said Walter Benjamin,[23] and the most significant contribution of research in the humanities and social sciences will lie in its power to ensure that questions remain open, debates remain alive and critique flourishes.

### Notes

1   Benjamin Jowet, quoted in Logan Pearsall Smith, *Unforgotten Years* (London, 1938). Cited in *Bloomsbury Thematic Dictionary of Quotations* (London: Bloomsbury, 1990), p.360.
2   Figure taken from the Australian Bureau of Statistics *Research and Experimental Development All-Sector Summary.*
3   See Trevor Haywood, *Info-Rich—Info-Poor: Access and Exchange in the Global Information Society* (London: Bowker Saur, 1995), p.87.
4   K.K. Ruthven, 'The Future of Disciplines: A Report on Ignorance,' in Australian Academy of the Humanities, *Knowing Ourselves and Others: The Humanities in Australia into the 21st Century* (Canberra: Australian Government Publishing Services, 1998), 3 vols, vol III. I am grateful to Professor Ruthven for allowing me to read and quote from an advance copy of his essay.

5    Cf Peter W. Sheehan, 'Research in the Humanities and Social Sciences.' Paper presented to the Deans of Arts and Social Sciences, Queensland University of Technology 3 July 1997, p.14.

6    Peter Sheldrake, 'Great Expectations: Education and the World of Work.' The 1997 A.W. Jones Lecture, Adelaide 26 April 1997, n.p. [pp.3-4]. See also Simon Marginson, *Education and Public Policy in Australia* (Cambridge: CUP, 1993), p.198.

7    Bill Gates with Nathan Myhrvold and Peter Rinearson, *The Road Ahead* (New York: Viking, 1995), p.6.

8    Harry Maddox, *Theory of Knowledge and its Dissemination* (Castlemaine: Freshet Press, 1993), p.3.

9    Sheldrake, 'Great Expectations,' [p.7].

10   John Milton, *Areopagitica*, in *John Milton,* ed. Stephen Orgel and Jonathan Goldberg, The Oxford Authors (Oxford: Oxford University Press, 1991), p.257.

11   For a discussion of metaphors in historical research, see Ann Curthoys, 'Opening Address: Thinking About History,' *Australian Historical Association Bulletin,* no. 83 (December, 1996), pp.14-28.

12   The phrase is taken from W.W. Bartley III, *Unfathomed Knowledge, Unmeasured Wealth: On Universities and the Wealth of Nations* (La Salle, Illinios: Open Court, 1990), p.24.

13   Ruthven, 'Future of Disciplines.'

14   Cf John Frow, 'Beyond the Disciplines: Cultural Studies,' in *Beyond the Disciplines: The New Humanities,* ed. K.K. Ruthven, Occasional Paper No. 13: Papers from the Australian Academy of the Humanities Symposium 1991 (Canberra: Australian Academy of the Humanities, 1992), p.25.

15   Jonathon Culler, *Framing the Sign: Criticism and its Institutions* (Oxford: Basil Blackwell, 1988), p.48.

16   Ruthven, 'Future of Disciplines'.

17   Marginson, *Education and Public Policy, passim.*

18    Michael Jackson, 'A Classical Case for Minding About What Matters,' *Campus Review,* 16–22 July 1997, p.12; and Rob Gilbert, 'Classic Comment,' *Campus Review,* 30 July–5 August 1997, p.12.

19   For a parallel defence of specialisation, see Culler, *Framing the Sign,* pp.53-55.

20   Terry Eagleton, 'Spaced Out', *London Review of Books,* 24 April 1997, p.22.

21   Ruthven, 'Future of Disciplines'.

22   Ann Curthoys, 'Unlocking the Academies: Responses and Strategies', *Meanjin,* 50 (1991), 391-92.

23   Walter Benjamin, Letter 9 December 1923 (pub. in *Briefe* no. 126, Frankfurt, 1966). Quoted in Susan Sontag, 'Under the Sign of Saturn', introductory essay to Benjamin's *One-Way Street and Other Writings* (1978); reprinted in Susan Sontag, *Under the Sign of Saturn* (New York: Farrar Straus Giroux, 1980), p.122.

*Graeme Hugo*

# Putting People Back into the Planning Process: The Changing Role of Geographical Information Systems

People must be at the *centre* of all social and economic planning, whether this be in the private or the public sector. It could be argued that much public policy and planning in Australia of recent decades has not been people-centred but driven by a range of other agendas. Resource allocation by government agencies has been increasingly based on a number of other principles including user pays, full cost recovery, cost effectiveness, benchmarking and of course a range of political considerations. Despite the widespread rhetoric of social justice, much of the resource allocation in our society is not done on the basis of an assessment of the needs of the majority of the people.

What I will argue here is that developments in *spatial information systems* can help not only in putting people back as the central focus of planning but also in assisting people to participate in the planning process itself. This may seem to go against conventional wisdom which would suggest that it has been advances in information technology which have helped depersonalise much of the social and economic activity we engage in during our daily lives. However, it is my conviction that in contrast to the 'big brother' image that information technology tends to attract, in contemporary developments in the area of information technology at the University of Adelaide, there is considerable potential for achieving a greater people focus in social and economic policy development and planning.

Graeme Hugo, Professor of Geography, has held visiting positions at the University of Iowa, University of Hawaii, Hasanuddin University (Indonesia), and the Australian National University; and has worked with a range of UN agencies, World Bank, World Fertility Survey, ILO, as well as Australian and South Australian government agencies. He is the author of some 100 books, articles and book-chapters, including: *Atlas of the Australian People 1991, National Overview* (AGPS) 1995; *Australian Immigration: A Survey of Issues* (AGPS) 1994, with M. Wooden, R. Holton and J. Sloan.

In addressing this issue I will draw upon work currently being carried out in the National Key Centre for Social Applications in GIS (known as GISCA) based in the Division of Humanities and Social Sciences at the University of Adelaide. What I will try to do is show how the application of Geographical Information Systems (GIS) or Spatial Information Systems (SIS) can be utilised to put people back into the planning process. My argument is that this can be done in two ways:

- Firstly by facilitating the incorporating of considerations of people, their characteristics and needs into each stage of the planning process.
- Secondly by facilitating the participation of people in the planning process itself.

Most attention will be focused on the first of these since it is in that area that the bulk of the Key Centre's work to date has been carried out. However, I will also make some comments on the use of GIS in actually involving communities directly in the planning process which is where we see much of our work in the near future.

At the outset I will explain what GIS is, or SIS as it is sometimes called, and also consider the ways it can be helpful in social planning. Then I will outline the work of the National Key Centre for Social Applications of GIS. I will try and explain the rationale for establishing the Key Centre which largely was based around the conviction that modern developments in GIS technology and methodology in Australia have not been brought to bear in areas of social and human service provision. It was argued that since these areas account for around a seventh of the total wealth generated in Australia, the potential of GIS to assist in obtaining more effective, equitable and efficient outcomes in the allocation of those resources should be explored. I will then move on to a brief consideration of some of the projects that the Key Centre has in progress or has recently completed which demonstrate how people can be better incorporated into the planning process. I will consider seven such projects. Next there will be a brief discussion of how we believe GIS can facilitate the participation of people into the planning process itself using some examples of our own work and that of others elsewhere in the world. In concluding I would like to raise a number of issues which I see as posing difficulties to the achievement of greater involvement of people in planning via the application of GIS. There are some significant barriers which threaten to compromise greatly the potential gains that GIS may bring in the area of public policy development and planning.

### What is GIS?

While the term 'information systems' is used very widely to include any set of data relating to a group of entities, more formally an information system is a set of processes executed on raw data to produce information which will be useful in decision making. It has two major elements:

- a facility for storing and retrieving information;

- an information system must also, however, have a full range of functions to handle observation, measurement, description, explanation, forecasting and decision making.

Spatial Information Systems are systems where the data in the system are spatially referenced. That is, in addition to the information which we have about any unit in the system (e.g. an individual, a property etc.) we know its location on the earth's surface. Hence it allows us not only to consider the characteristics of that unit but also those of its location and immediate vicinity, and we can consider its location in relation to other units, e.g. household locations in relation to the nearest medical facility.

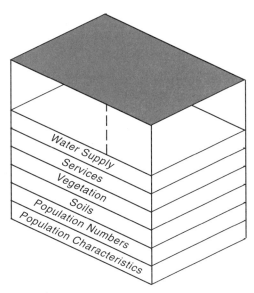

Figure 1. A simplified model of a geographical information system

A Spatial Information System can be conceptualised as a series of layers of information with each observation in each layer tied to specific points and areas on the earth's surface via a specific latitude and longitude (Figure 1). Figure 2 shows that Spatial Information Systems can be divided into three types.[1]

- Computer Assisted Drawing (CAD)—graphical systems which support the work of engineers, architects, industrial designers. It involves largely data collection, manipulation, visualisation and presentation.

- Land Information Systems (LIS)—primarily a tool for the legal, administrative and economic management of land resources. It consists of:

  - a database containing spatially referenced land-related data (particularly land parcels and spatial networks);

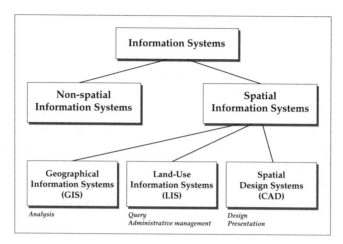

Figure 2. A classification of (Spatial) Information Systems
Source: Scholten and Van der Vlugt 1990

- a set of procedures and techniques for the systematic collection, updating and querying of data.

Only minimal spatial analysis is involved and it is used widely in local government, water, electricity and other public utilities and telecommunications.

- Geographical Information Systems (GIS)—a tool for urban and regional research, policy analysis, policy simulation and planning. It contains three elements:

  - a database containing spatially referenced data;

  - a set of procedures for data collection, update and query;

  - procedures for spatial analysis, modelling, policy evaluation and optimisation and elaborate cartographic display functions.

There is a growing realisation that almost all government and private sector activities would gain from having their information systems spatially referenced since it provides much greater scope for using those data bases to improve decision making. As a result, expertise in SIS and GIS is becoming an increasingly important qualification for jobs across a range of private and public sector areas. The State government of South Australia has identified this as one of the strategic areas for future economic development of the State and aims for South Australia to lead not only Australia in the SIS area but also the whole Asia-Pacific region.

### The role of GIS in social planning

What role can GIS play in assisting the decision making process of social planners? This area has not been widely discussed in the literature and the following summary is drawn largely from Page, Hugo, Worrall, Plane and Rogerson, Coucelis, and Conning.[2] Before examining some of the potential areas where GIS can be helpful in social planning, it is important to consider how resources are presently allocated by government agencies in Australia.

State government in the Australian system has much of the responsibility for delivering services at the community level. The bulk of state budgets are allocated to the provision of education, health, social and community services through allocation of resources to pay for staff, buildings, etc. in communities throughout the metropolitan and non-metropolitan parts of the state. Accordingly, the issue of how resources are allocated between communities is of critical significance in the budgeting process. Obviously in an era of considerable budgeting constraint the competition for scarce resources is considerable and there are a number of principles which can be adopted in allocating resources between communities. Much of the contemporary rhetoric argues that allocation of many resources by government should be needs-based and hence take into account the extent of dis-advantage among groups and areas. However, in reality the principles of resource allocation tend to be one of the following:

- a fixed allocation to each community or area;

- a *per capita* approach whereby resources are allocated according to the num-ber of residents in an area;

- a response-based approach whereby resources are provided in response to submissions or pressure and lobbying from communities;

- a demand-based approach whereby resources are provided according to cur-rent rates of usage of particular services;

- a history-based approach whereby services are provided according to how they have been provided in the past;

- a needs-based approach whereby the level of need in an area for a particular service is established using some benchmarking procedure.

Analyses of the existing situation in Australia indicate that while in reality it is often a mixture of these principles which are adopted by government departments or agencies in allocating their resources, genuine needs-based allocations are limited.

How can GIS be of assistance in this area? Most importantly GIS can help con-siderably in social planning in *diagnosing social conditions and needs*. Page argues that:

> In the larger scheme of program planning and evaluation research, GIS contributions to the identification of human and social needs may be very critical. GIS doesn't do this by mobilising the alienated, the poor and un-employed. Rather it contributes mainly in mundane, but essential ways, by

applying its techniques to identify existing circumstances and needs and forecast the emergence of new ones, and describing with precision the sizes and
locations of problems currently and prospectively requiring attention.[3]

He makes the very important point that GIS can diagnose community distress
and define the clients of proposed interventions through systematic and repro-
ducible procedures and hence avoid action being initiated by policy makers in
response to lobbying pressure, speculation, impressionistic observation and even
biased information. If we are to move to a needs-of-people-based planning model
rather than one responding only to agitation, political lobbying and community
pressures on decision makers, the timely availability of accurate and relevant
information for areas is of fundamental importance.

Demand and need for all goods and services are not evenly distributed across
all subgroups of the population and across all areas. Moreover, as the population
changes the nature and level of that demand and need will also change. However,
demand and need are influenced by a range of individual characteristics of which
age and income are recognised as being the most important.[4] The overlaying function of GIS allows each of the characteristics of populations relevant to the need
or demand for a particular good or service to be taken into account in producing
a map of consumer demand. Here the approach is to identify particular target
groups by detailed field and/or market segments and then use census data to establish their spatial distribution. In the commercial world this makes it possible 'to
segment the initial selling area into a number of smaller areas where it is hoped
the highest levels of response to either direct mail or some form of advertising will
be achieved'.[5] This process of relating knowledge of market segmentation to spatial
distribution of population with different characteristics is a major commercial
application of GIS.

The capacity of GIS to overlay spatial distributions of subgroups of population
and the network of existing supply points of goods and services which the
populations access is an important potential use of GIS in local and state government. One area where there is considerable need to exploit this potential is in the
provision of services to the elderly population. The elderly are the fastest growing
segment of the Australian population and are very intensive users of health and
other services. Moreover, they often are very restricted in their mobility. Hence
in planning the location of services to the elderly it is important that their
accessibility to the older population be maximised. Similarly in a constrained
economic situation it is important to maximise cost efficiency in the provision of
those services. A GIS which overlays the distribution of the current older population (and also perhaps that of 5-10 years hence), the existing service delivery
points and the existing public transport/community bus routes, etc. would greatly
assist in local and state government provision of health and community care,
meals on wheels, etc.

One of the most important and useful functions of GIS is its ability to act as an integrator of vastly different and complex spatially referenced data sets. In this context it is important to recognise that there are many concepts relating to population which are of significance in social and economic planning which are complex and multidimensional and not capturable in a single variable. These include such concepts as socio-economic status, underclass, economic and social well-being, disadvantage, ethnicity, multiculturalism, deprivation, vulnerability and locational disadvantage.

Obviously these concepts are of fundamental significance in achieving important government objectives of equity and social justice. Unfortunately accurate measurement and calibration of concepts such as those mentioned above in small areas is not readily achieved in a single variable. They are complex multi-dimensional concepts. Clearly the overlaying function of GIS is relevant here. Overlaying two or more relevant coverages or several individual map layers allows all the dimensions of the concepts to be captured in a single new coverage. This is a new base file made up of areas resulting from the superimposition of areas on the original maps using user-defined rules of union and interaction.[6]

The function of GIS in facilitating the development of measures of important and useful concepts for planners also extends to its ability

> to make operational certain specific locational concepts and techniques: these concepts include the systematic analysis of proximity, accessibility, connectivity and density. In addition, GIS can also perform traditional locational analysis. The effective integration of all these functions and facilities would be very difficult to achieve, if not impossible, using traditional (i.e. non-GIS) methods.[12]

The facility of GIS to make sophisticated measures of accessibility is especially important from the policy-making and planning perspective. Distances between sales and service delivery points and the households and other units they serve can be calculated in a range of ways. Distance can be measured in 'crow flies' distance or a more functionally appropriate measure like road distance or travel time. There are many examples of this use of GIS. A study by Ng and Wilkins[8] analyses the distance of all postal code areas in Canada from the nearest hospital facility. A Costa Rican study[9] uses GIS to estimate physical accessibility to health services in communities across the island using the concept of population potential. It was able to identify the most under-serviced areas and hence make clear-cut recommendations regarding the opening of new facilities.

Another major area where GIS can play a major role in the effective and equitable provision of social services applies *after* decisions to provide services have been made. This lies in the monitoring and evaluation of the effectiveness of that provision. Increasingly, government agencies are being required to benchmark their provision of services against national and international standards. GIS provides a methodology and technology to facilitate such assessments in a timely and objective way. This is of crucial importance because

- The populations of areas are in a constant state of change so that the nature and extent of need in an area will also be subject to continual change.

- If provision of services is effective it should reduce the extent of need in the area where they are deployed. GIS can assist in the evaluation of how well programs are operating, in particular areas by monitoring changes in the conditions in those areas which the programs are aimed at addressing.

Hence it is argued that GIS has the potential for improving the planning, design, operation, management and evaluation of delivery of a wide range of health, education and other social services after the decisions have been made about how resources are allocated between areas. Page has summarised the benefits which GIS offers in this respect as follows:

- *Earlier needs detection.* A geographic information system normally provides the easiest and quickest way to track and diagnose ever-changing social pathologies, which after initial identification, serve as the basis for government assistance.

- *Quicker conflict resolution.* The clarity of well-designed maps enables the discussion at key meetings to focus on how to tackle problems, rather than on debating whether or where a problem exists. A clearer understanding of the issues results in better strategic decision making.

- *Better financial planning.* Well-implemented geographical information systems have the ability to highlight areas where resources are deficient, in terms of either the overall needs of target populations or in addressing the needs of particular segments of the designated population.

- *Continual monitoring.* Often, after only a few months' time, the social problem being addressed by a government program may change in substantial ways while the programs and services designed to control the problem have not. Ongoing monitoring of social conditions can alert decision makers to the need to reorient program activities to fit changing circumstances.

- *Reassessment and evaluation.* Most program managers have few additional resources available to evaluate the effectiveness of their programs. GIS is valuable because it allows long-term evaluation of how well a program is operating by matching the needs with the services in a manner that is subordinate to the actual service provision.[10]

Modern developments in Geographical Information Systems (GIS) have made possible better organisation and analysis of spatially referenced data to support state service programming in a wide range of areas. Effective use of GIS technology and techniques can enhance the performance of agencies and programs and offer the means to achieve a greater 'people' orientation in planning and in doing so improve the development, analysis and implementation of public policy so that more effective and equitable allocations of scarce resources and more sustainable uses of the environment are achieved. Similarly GIS has much to offer the private sector in producing or delivering goods and services to the community in more cost-efficient and profitable ways, taking into account the need to use the environment in a sustainable way. However, in Australia this potential has not been realised. Some years ago Gamer, in observing that the application of Geographical Information Systems (GIS) was well established in both the public and private sectors in Australia, noted that this was

> particularly the case in the area of LIS and in natural resource and environ-
> mental management but less so for social, economic and planning implica-
> tions—these are areas in which developments are still at a relatively early
> stage compared with other countries.[11]

Although some progress has been made, Gamer's assessment remains essentially accurate. Although GIS has been used more widely in social planning in both North America and Europe, there remains considerable debate in the literature about the extent to which GIS has been able to contribute in the planning process. Among the criticisms levelled at GIS, the following are most important in this context:

- GIS has had more impact on 'lower order' planning activities (e.g. engineer-
  ing, spatial design) than on higher order activities such as strategic planning
  and policy making.[12]

- GIS has been used more as a means of sophisticated mapping than as an
  analytical tool.[13]

One of the contentions on which the Key Centre is based is that the incorporation of population, social and economic variables into GIS assists in over-
coming these criticisms. This is partly because inclusion of population into these systems immediately gives them a relevance to strategic planning and policy-
making since people are rightfully the central focus of most planning.

### National Key Centre for social applications of GIS

Key Centres are a national program of the Australian Research Council (ARC) designed to set up a number of Centres of Excellence in Research and Teaching in Australian universities. The Program was established in 1995 with the following objectives:

- to significantly enhance the quantity and quality of teaching and research in
  higher education;

- to improve the higher education sector's capacity to provide expertise in
  areas relevant to national, economic, technological and social goals;

- to strengthen and promote cooperation between higher education and industry and user groups;

- to promote the interrelationship of teaching and research and develop inter-disciplinary links and programs in host institutions.

Obtaining funding for the Centres is extremely competitive and only three submissions can be made by each university across all disciplines. In the 1995 round only seven were funded from more than ninety applications and one of them was the National Key Centre for Social Applications of GIS at the University of Adelaide.

The idea behind the Centre is that in Australia we have not taken advantage of modern developments in GIS methodology and technology to assist in planning the delivery of goods and services in the public and private sectors. It was argued that GIS can assist in developing resource allocation strategies which maximise equity, cost efficiency and profitability. The detailed vision and objectives of the Key Centre are presented in Table 1.

### Table 1. National Key Centre for Social Applications of GIS: Vision and Objectives

**VISION AND OBJECTIVES**

**Vision**
Our vision is to become an international leader in the application of GIS technologies to social and community planning programs.

**Centre Objectives**
- To provide a major focus and vehicle for researchers and planners to collaborate in the analysis and use of population and social data.

- To make public and private sector planning in Australia 'smarter' through the effective incorporation of existing data using advanced geographic information technology into research in changing patterns of need as well as into the planning process in an effective and timely way.

- To undertake basic and applied research that will facilitate the incorporation of social and demographic data using GIS technology into planning in a more timely and effective way.

- To develop new technologies in GIS.

- To provide education and training in the use of social and demographic data in planning, and the application of GIS to social planning issues.

Table 2. National Key Centre for Social Applications of GIS:
Core Partners

| CORE PARTNERS | |
| --- | --- |
| University of Adelaide | |
| University of South Australia | RESEARCH |
| Flinders University of S.A. | |
| Australian Bureau of Statistics | |
| Department of Environment and | DATA PROVIDERS |
| Natural Resources | |
| Department of Housing and | |
| Urban Development | APPLICATION |

Table 3. National Key Centre for Social Applications of GIS:
Supporting Partners

| SUPPORTING PARTNERS | |
| --- | --- |
| ESRI Pty Ltd | |
| MAPTEK Pty Ltd | SOFTWARE SUPPLIERS |
| Formida | |
| Computer Associates | |
| Silicon Graphics Corporation | HARDWARE SUPPLIERS |
| Communica Systems | TRAINERS |
| Kinhill Engineers | |
| Coded Australia | |
| Space Time Research | CONSULTANTS |
| Daedalus SA Pty Ltd | |
| Spatial Concepts Pty Ltd | |
| South Australian Heath Commission | |
| Local Government Association | GOVERNMENT AGENCIES |
| Commission for the Ageing | |

Although the University of Adelaide was the lead agency in developing the Key
Centre proposal it actually came into being from an existing informal relationship
between the University and several South Australian government agencies. The
Centre is emphatically a cooperative activity involving a number of core partners

(Table 2) and supporting partners (Table 3) drawn from the University, public and private sectors. The Centre had been established for 18 months [in August 1997] and had already established a significant national and international reputation, has a staff of 17 and derives the great majority of its funding from outside the University. It has both teaching and research functions although it is mainly the research activities which are reported on here. We are involved not only in teaching at university level in all three universities in Adelaide but also are attempting to get GIS established in South Australian schools.

The Centre also sees itself as playing a significant role in the State government's strategy of making Adelaide a major centre of the spatial information industry in the Asia-Pacific region. The State government's strategy involves attracting a major international company to establish a significant part of its regional operations in Adelaide in return for obtaining the State government's Spatial Information Systems business. For this industry to be successful in Adelaide the Key Centre can provide two crucially important ingredients:

- A research and development capacity.

- Production of high quality human resources to support the industry.

Hence the Key Centre sees it as being crucially important that it encourage and support teaching of GIS at all levels and carry out research of the highest quality in both pure and applied areas. In all of these respects it is necessary for the Key Centre to keep a close relationship with the Spatial Information industry so that it is able to respond in a timely way to the needs of the industry in both research and teaching.

### Some examples of putting people back into planning using GIS
I will now turn to a brief examination of a number of projects currently under way in the Key Centre which illustrate how GIS can be used to put people back into the planning process. More details of these projects can be obtained from the Key Centre's Home Page (http://www.gisca.adelaide.edu.au). The examples are drawn from the work of a range of individual researchers in the Centre drawn from the various research clusters established in the Centre (Table 4).

### Indicators of disadvantage
There are a number of projects in the Key Centre which are investigating the extent to which there is an increasing spatial polarisation in Australian cities and non-metropolitan areas.

The objective of these studies is to establish the spatial impact of the economic and social restructuring of the last two decades in Australia and test the hypothesis that there has been an increase in inequality. There is growing evidence in all of the OECD countries that there has been a 'hollowing out' of the middle class

**Table 4. National Key Centre for Social Applications of GIS:
Research Clusters**

| RESEARCH CLUSTERS |
| --- |
| Population Dynamics |
| Community Planning |
| Environment and Legal |
| New Technologies in Spatial Information |
| Geodemographic Database |

and growth of higher and lower income groups. It has been suggested that these increasingly polarised two groups are becoming increasingly spatially separated within our cities and non-metropolitan areas. The aim of this work in the Key Centre is to develop indicators to chart the changes in spatial patterns of disadvantage and establish what the implications are for allocating resources and providing services to ameliorate these differences.

These studies have as a basic premise that there is a complex interdependence and interplay between the people forming a local community and the actual location or place in which they live.[14] The issue of locational disadvantage has attracted considerable attention among researchers and policy makers in Australia during the 1990s. The term has become widely used and although it has been interpreted somewhat differently by different groups its essence is captured in the following quotation from the policy maker most responsible for bringing it to prominence in the public policy agenda, the former Deputy Prime Minister Mr Brian Howe (in the foreword to Maher):

> Disadvantages can arise where people have limited access to services and recreational facilities or have poor employment, training and educational opportunities because of where they live. Locational disadvantages can reduce the quality of life for many Australians and can exacerbate other disadvantages, especially those associated with low income.
> Locational disadvantage is increasingly being recognised as a major social issue. Australians living in major cities, in rural and remote areas, often experience inequities in access to employment, affordable housing, public transport and public services and facilities.[15]

Issues of spatial inequality and locational disadvantage within Australia have been the subject of research since the 1960s.[16] However, in recent times the debate has increased in intensity for a number of reasons. There is an increasing amount of evidence of an increasing polarisation between rich and poor in Australia's major cities.[17] While there is debate about the extent and nature of the inequality[18] the evidence would suggest that, not only within Australia but also within several OECD nations, there is an increasing polarisation between better-off and poor and that this has an important spatial dimension. Indeed there appears to have been a sharpening of differences between poor and well-off areas within large cities; and that real incomes have fallen in poor areas while they have increased in the better off parts of cities.[19] More controversially, it has been suggested by some that the increasing spatial concentration of poverty is in itself exacerbating in some way the deprivation of people living in those areas so that they are less influenced than other urban residents by upturns in the economy or macro economic interventions designed to ease unemployment. Accordingly it has been suggested that there is a need to focus specifically upon these economically distressed areas and develop distinctive policy and program interventions to improve conditions within those areas. Whereas in the past much of the interest in spatial inequality has focused upon Australia's major cities, the revival of interest in this issue in the 1990s has also focused upon non-metropolitan Australia. This is part of a growth in the regional movement as a third force in Australian public policy (to the federal and state governments).

Hence issues of regional disadvantage and locational disadvantage in regional cities and rural and remote Australia have assumed much greater prominence.[20] Moreover, it has been argued that there is increasing spatial polarisation evident in non-metropolitan Australia.[21]

The work of the Key Centre in these areas is first of all in developing indicators to show trends in disadvantage at small area level. The patterns depicted for Adelaide in Figure 3 are illustrative of the types of maps that can be produced for single variables and Figure 4 shows the types of composite variables that can be depicted. Our focus, however, is upon analysing trends over time in these patterns, explaining them and what are the implications for allocating resources and providing services.

### Access to education services

A major theme of work in the Key Centre relates to the equitable and efficient provision of education services. Access to education is a fundamental element in social well being and GIS can be used to:

- establish areas where participation in various levels of education is above or below national averages;

- areas where physical accessibility to various levels of education are low;

- establish optimal locations of new educational facilities so that accessibility to the largest number of potential students is maximised;

- establish where school closures will have the least overall impact.

A simple example of the type of analysis that can be undertaken is provided in Figure 5 which shows the distribution of the places of origin of students at the University of Adelaide in 1996.

It can be seen when this distribution is compared with the distribution of all 15-24 year olds in Adelaide (taken to represent the population from which the University student population is drawn) that there are some significant differences. Clearly the University is not drawing anything like the proportionate share of its students from the lower socioeconomic status suburbs of the northern and southern parts of the Adelaide Metropolitan Area. These are obviously areas in which the University should focus its access and equity policies and programs.

### Access to health services
GIS can be used in a similar way in health planning as it can in education planning, although it also can be used in additional ways in epidemiology to examine the spread of diseases and in environmental health. The example we have used here is depicted in Figure 6 which is drawn from a study which the Key Centre undertook for the Victorian government. This was a study of service provision in the Hume region in the northeastern part of the state. The objective was to identify variations in degrees of access to specific types of medical services such as emergency, intensive care and maternity services. This was to be used as a basis for planning location of new services and provision of specialised transport services for people in the most disadvantaged areas.

### Establishing the support base of the Adelaide Crows
The Key Centre has been involved in a number of studies which have assisted sporting clubs. These have included an analysis of the distribution of people involved in bowling clubs. We have also assisted the South Australian National Football League in determining the boundaries for areas within which clubs can recruit players. We were approached by the Adelaide Football Club to analyse its support base. They had a number of objectives, one of which was to test the commonly held view that it is a club of the 'Chardonnay-set' or yuppies.

However, our analysis showed that the overwhelming support for the club came from young families located in the growing northern and southern suburbs. The club was thus able to use this in developing its image as 'the club for all South Australians' but also for targeting junior development activity.

### Anticipating population growth
A major focus of the Key Centre from its earliest days has been to develop more accurate population forecasts at small area level to assist in more timely and cost effective planning of services. We have completed a number of studies which use GIS to link traditional demographic methods which make assumptions concerning future fertility, mortality and migration trends and knowledge in the housing market and land development. Effective urban planning requires physical infrastructure and human services to be provided in the right place at the right time and this can only be achieved if we have detailed and relatively accurate forecasts

Figure 3. Metropolitan Adelaide: low income families^ as a percentage of all families in each postcode, 1991
Source: Glover, Shand, Forster and Woollacott 1996

N

17.0 per cent of families^ in Metropolitan Adelaide at 6 August 1991 had an annual income of $16,000 or less

Percentage of low income families^

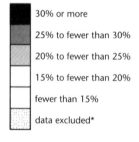

30% or more

25% to fewer than 30%

20% to fewer than 25%

15% to fewer than 20%

fewer than 15%

data excluded*

Percentage of low income families^

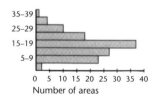

35–39
25–29
15–19
5–9

0   5  10 15 20 25 30 35 40
Number of areas

^   Families with annual income of $16,000 or less as a percentage of all families for which income information was obtained

*   Data was excluded because either too many non-resident persons were included in the Census, the postcode population is fewer than 100, or only a small part of the postcode is located in Metropolitan Adelaide.

Note:
Overlaid boundaries are statistical local areas

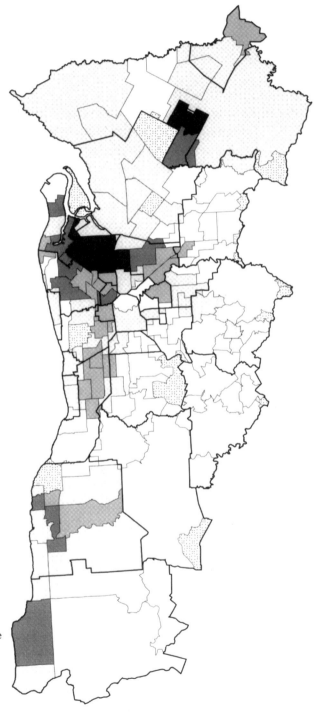

Figure 4. Metropolitan Adelaide: clusters of postcodes with generally similar socio-economic characteristics, 1991
Source: Glover, Shand, Forster and Woollacott 1996

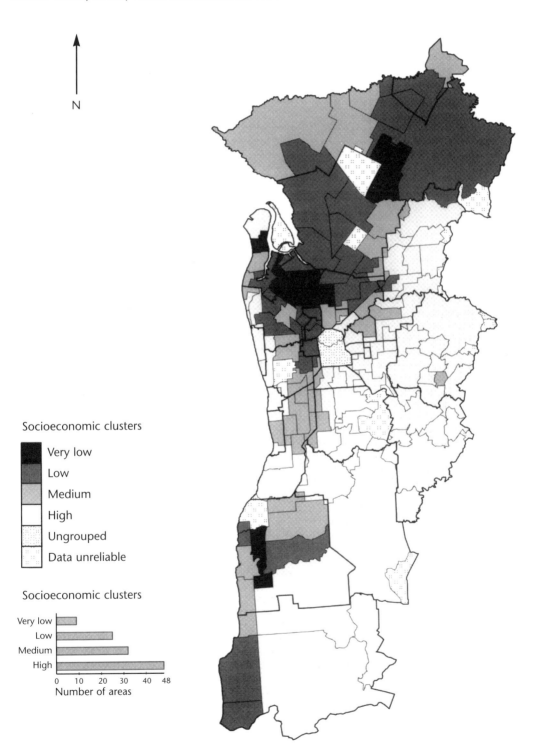

Figure 5. Adelaide: percentage of population in census collectors' districts aged 15–24 and
University of Adelaide students as a percentage of total population aged 15–24, 1996
Source: ABS 1996 Census and University of Adelaide enrolment statistics

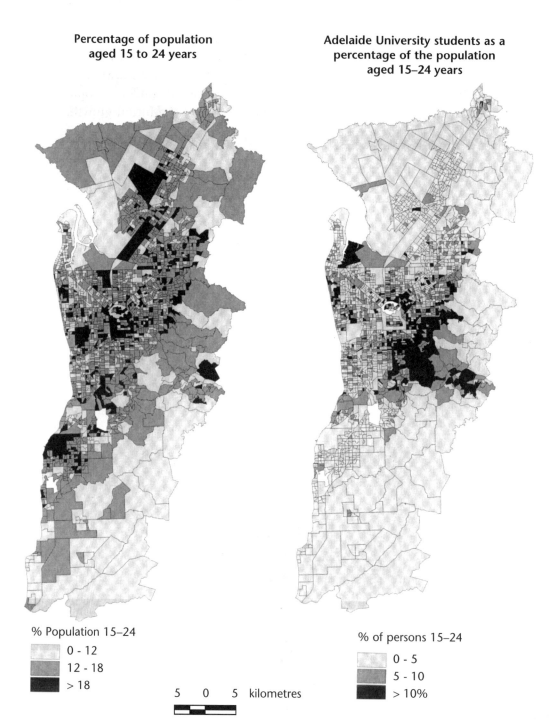

Percentage of population
aged 15 to 24 years

Adelaide University students as a
percentage of the population
aged 15–24 years

% Population 15–24

   0 - 12

   12 - 18

   > 18

5    0    5   kilometres

% of persons 15–24

   0 - 5

   5 - 10

   > 10%

of population change and housing construction at the local level. One of the Key Centre's major research projects involves the development of such forecasting techniques. One example is by Bell, Nicolson, Blake and McQueen.[22] What we have done is to bring together a small area-land use model and broader demographic forecasting to produce a flexible forecasting methodology for Adelaide. The example is of Noarlunga local government area and in this case the forecast population change over the 1991-2001 period is animated and shows how some of the built-up areas around Noarlunga Town Centre will undergo population decline and other areas on the periphery will experience significant growth.

## Assessing insurance risk

One of the most outstanding projects of the Key Centre in its short history is the development of a Three Dimensional Model of the Adelaide City Area. This was developed by one of our researchers, Dr Stephen Kirkby, in collaboration with one of our commercial partners, Maptek. The Adelaide 3D GIS planning model is a three dimensional representation of all buildings and infrastructure in Adelaide. This allows planners to immerse themselves in the Adelaide environment and

Figure 6. Hume area of Victoria: Accessibility to urban centres with hospitals.
Source: Rudd and Nicholson 1997

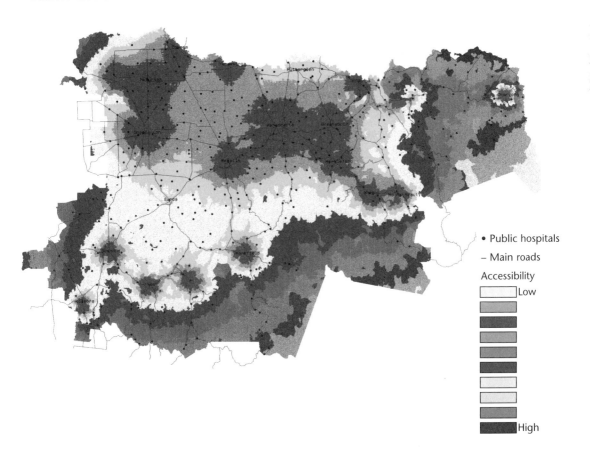

position themselves anywhere within the 3D space to view in any direction any aspect of the city. It also allows us to change any aspect of the city's structure in the model and see what the ramifications of that change are. We can model any physical, economic, social or demographic change and see how it will impact on the city. The data incorporated in the model are from government agencies and so far include buildings, building details, property boundaries, roads, water mains, storm-water, sewerage and electricity cables. We were invited as the only university representative to present the model at the Australian government stand at the UN Habitat Conference in Istanbul in 1996. It is the only model of its kind in the world and has attracted international attention. For example, we subsequently reached agreement with the Geographical Survey Institute in Japan to build a comparable model for a city in Japan. This study was launched at the Australian Embassy in Tokyo in November 1997.

One example of the way in which the model can be used is this. We were approached by Sedgwick, an insurance company with 2000 offices worldwide. They had the task of assessing the insurance risk for all government buildings in Adelaide. They had planned to bring out three engineers for three months from California to do the task. Using the 3D model, all the work was done from the California office and one engineer came for one month—a total saving of $300,000.

With this combination of GIS and the Internet we now have an incredibly powerful tool for dissemination of information, technology that is now available today can be used to assist people make a more informed decision and in a much more cost effective way.

### Responding to bushfire

Another project developed as part of the fruitful collaboration of the Key Centre with Maptek involves an emergency planning GIS for dynamic fire modelling across the Internet. The model is built on a CSIRO fire model. This was well described in an article in the *Australian Financial Review*:

> A fire is raging through dry vegetation in the Adelaide hills and strong gusts of wind from the west are spreading the flames close to a group of homes on the edge of the bush.
>
> At the scene, police are evacuating homes. But suddenly the wind changes direction and a residential area that was safe just minutes ago is now under threat.
>
> What are the police to do?
>
> Today these police must rely on their own abilities to assess which direction to send people who are being evacuated.
>
> But police of the future will be able to use an Internet-based system to antic-ipate changes in the fire.
>
> South Australian police have been talking to the developers of a prototype geographic information system—developed by the University of Adelaide—designed to simulate fires.

The software will allow emergency personnel to enter conditions such as wind speed and direction, temperature and humidity into a laptop in the field and match this with topographical information already in the system. The information can be relayed back to the central command via mobile phone so that decisions can be made immediately about where to deploy resources and what alternatives are available.

Information is updated as conditions change.

This will let police anticipate changes in the fire based on weather and topographical conditions—or, in their hunt for arsonists, even track the spread of a fire to assess where it started.

The computer system will be a big leap forward for the emergency services in terms of monitoring the development of fires, cutting down cost and time in responding to a crisis and saving lives.[23]

### Involving people in the planning process

One of the developments in GIS in recent years is to link it to the Internet so that more people can gain access to the information and results of analysis within a GIS. This has the potential for the wider community participating in the planning process and opens up the possibilities of placing more information into the hands of the community. This not only has the potential to allow individuals and communities to make better informed decisions about their own behaviours but also provides them with the information to be more active in community planning and to be better informed about developments in their own community. With the roll-out of cables to a large proportion of Australian houses for Cable TV, access to the Internet will be possible for the majority of Australian homes. Moreover, with advancing satellite technology the ability for households to access relevant information systems from home will be greatly enhanced. People will be able to click on their own home area and access relevant information about it. This whole process is possible now and is only being held back by lack of open public access to relevant data sets. At the Key Centre we have begun to explore some of the possibilities in this area.

### Eco-tourism

One of the earliest projects undertaken by the Key Centre involved Eco-Tourism. This involved setting up a GIS of information on a range of eco-tourist destinations within the Southeast region of South Australia. Through the Internet potential tourists could readily access the information in the GIS about each of these destinations to inform their decisions about which areas to go to and what activities to carry out at the destinations.

### Friends of the Earth

An interesting overseas example of how GIS technology can empower communities is the website of the Friends of the Earth in the United Kingdom. What this allows people to do is to click on their home area and establish exactly what the level of various kinds of pollution is in the area. This allows people to take appropriate

actions such as organising opposition and lobbying groups or in terms of particular strategies to minimise the detrimental effects of the pollution. Hence by
linking the GIS and Internet technologies, the public are given high levels of
accessibility to appropriate information.

### Secondary education in Indonesia

One of the major objectives in the Key Centre has been to internationalise our
research and teaching activities. As part of this process we have strategically
targeted three countries in Asia—China, Japan and Indonesia—and have a number of activities in each country. One of particular interest in the current context
involves a pilot project in planning an expansion of secondary schools in
Indonesia. As part of its Sixth and Seventh Five Year Plans the Indonesian government has aimed to have all Indonesian children stay at school to the end of Year
9. Currently schooling is compulsory only up to the end of Primary School (SD)
or Year 6. This will involve a massive construction of secondary schools to meet a
doubling of demand. It has been proposed that a GIS be set up to ensure that the
new schools be established in the most equitable and cost-efficient manner.

It should be mentioned that due to the fall in fertility which began in the early
1970s, and has seen the Total Fertility Rate fall from around 5.6 in the late 1970s
to around 2.8 in the early 1990s, the numbers beginning primary school should
start to reduce in the early years of next century and may have already begun to
do so. Accordingly, the strategy of the Department of Education is not only to
build new SMP (Junior Secondary Schools) but also to

- Expand existing SMP.

- Convert some excess SD to SMP.

- Add SMP to some selected SDs.

This all needs to be done in such a way as to maximise equity and efficiency.
It is proposed that a GIS prototype be developed for the province of West Java with
the aim of developing a methodology that would eventually be applied to other
provinces. The GIS would comprise the following layers of information:

- 1990 Census age/sex data by kecamatan and desa if possible.

- 1995 Intercensal Survey age/sex data by kabupaten.

- All roads & public transport

- Location of existing SD.

- Location of existing SMP and other lower secondary schools.

- Location of existing SMA and other higher secondary schools.

- Topography.

- Desa, kabupaten boundaries.

- Data on size of schools in terms of pupils by class and number of teachers.

Some features of the GIS would be:

- A facility to calculate accessibility from the centroid of each desa to the nearest SMP.

- A projection facility which will allow projection of the 1990 population ahead 20 years, so that secondary-school-age-children numbers can be estimated for the present and ahead some 10 years.

- 1995 SUPAS kabupaten data can be used to check the validity of the projections.[24]

The plan is to take the solutions obtained for expanding secondary school provision in terms of new schools and expansion of schools into the local communities to be effected by them. Hence part of the pilot survey will be taking the GIS into local communities and showing people where the planned developments would take place and get feedback about the GIS derived solutions. A key objective is to empower local communities by having them involved in the final decision of where the new educational facilities will be located.

### Barriers to greater use of GIS in social planning

In considering all of the developments and possibilities for GIS to increase the people orientation of social planning, it is relevant to recognise that there are a number of important issues which threaten to prevent that full potential being realised. Some of these will be briefly addressed here.

There are clearly important *confidentiality* considerations involved in the development of Spatial Information Systems which involve data relating to individuals being traceable to particular addresses. Such information systems are subject to abuse and unjustifiable intrusion by the state and private sector into the privacy of individuals. There needs to be developed clear codes of practice in the development and use of GIS which contain individual person and household information. There has been quite a lot of work done in developing safeguards within GIS to now allow such individual information to be derived from data sets but confidentiality issues remain of considerable concern.

It is largely in the *government sector* that confidentiality considerations have prevented the development of spatially referenced unit record data sets. Indeed, it is the main barrier preventing the Australian Bureau of Statistics geocoding all of their data sets, although some geocoding of industrial and agricultural data has already begun. A decision has not yet been taken about geocoding the 2001 Census of Population and Housing and it is confidentiality as well as cost that are seen as the main stumbling blocks. However, while the ABS does not genocode its data or at least produce data for smaller units than the current census collectors' district as is done in Canada (the blockfaceA) and New Zealand (the meshblock), it is unable to provide data for customised small areal units for users. This contrasts not only with their colleagues in the census and statistics agencies in countries like Canada and New Zealand, but also the private sector.

Increasingly, in the private sector extensive SIS are being developed using credit and transaction data, other financial transaction data, magazine and organisation subscriptions, etc. To develop individual-level spatially-referenced data bases in order to support direct mailing, telephone selling, credit rating checks, etc, increasingly, private sector users of small area data are turning to such data sets as opposed to the official systems developed by ABS because of the former's flexibility. It is clear that this is necessary to have workable and effective codes of practice for both government and private information systems if abuse of the technology is to be prevented. At present the restrictions imposed on the ABS, or perceived by the ABS to limit their activity, are simply driving the development of private sector data agencies which are not prevented from releasing individual level information to paying customers. It is possible to preserve individual confidentiality in Spatial Information Systems and the proper legislation and codes of practice need to be put in place to ensure that both the public and private sectors adopt those practices.

There are other considerations which also are a matter of concern and one relates to the availability of small-area data. The Australian Census of Population and Housing collects some of the world's most comprehensive and accurate small area data on the characteristics of population and housing down to the collectors' district level. However, increasingly, the cost-recovery policy of the Australian Bureau of Statistics means that these data are not accessible to many in the community. It is paradoxical that just when we have the technology to readily access and analyse the collectors' district level information from censuses, many groups are disenfranchised from accessing it because of the cost and/or lack of technical expertise to use the various census products. If the technology is to lead to a new more people-centred social planning, data sets need to be made both financially and technically accessible to the full spectrum of the community and not become the preserve of the wealthy and powerful.

A related issue refers to the relative importance given by official data collection authorities to the community level in dissemination of data. If the local and regional community is to become empowered by having access to relevant data, that information has to be made available in *spatial units* which are relevant to community needs. The ABS and other government agencies are guided in this area by the Australian Standard Geographical Classification (ASGC). This is depicted in

Figure 7 and it can be seen that the standard unit for community level analysis is the Statistical Local Area (SLA) which is predominantly made up of Local Government Areas (LGAs). It is apparent, however, that while LGAs certainly do have some relevance as data dissemination units they rarely represent local communities of interest and their boundaries are constantly changing. A recent internal review of the ASGC[25] recommended a radical restructuring of the ASGC, although it retained the LGA as an important unit of data dissemination. The restructuring is depicted in Figure 8 and among other elements it suggested that a new spatial unit be included in the ASGC—the statistical locality (SL). This would conform to suburbs in large urban areas and community of interest areas in non-metropolitan areas. This apparently has been rejected out of hand by senior ABS authorities so it will not be possible for communities to access ABS information in that form unless the boundaries of suburbs and country communities correspond with CD boundaries, which they rarely do.

In GIS, as in all technology, there is a real danger that the elite will gain control of it and that access among the mass of the community will remain limited. This must be guarded against especially since the technology and methodology of GIS, as in other areas involving computers, is becoming cheaper and more user-friendly and not necessitating years of training to interface with and use. There are two strategies which need to be pursued here if the vision of GIS becoming a way of involving people more in the planning process is to be realised. The first relates to South Australia's schools. If this State is to have SIS as an important part of its development strategy, training in the area must begin in the State's secondary schools. The Key Centre has recently been attempting to develop GIS as part of the Year 12 syllabus in Geography and train teachers in the relevant skills, but has met several barriers in this process. Firstly there is a reluctance to put GIS in the official syllabus because of great inequalities between schools in the availability of relevant hardware and software. This is an important argument because it means that schools in poorer areas are likely not to be able to access training in GIS and children from such areas will thus find it more difficult to pursue a career in SIS or access SIS in their day-to-day future lives as adults. Clearly, an equalisation of access to computers across SA schools is a non-negotiable priority if there is to be any pretence toward equity and social justice in the South Australian schooling system. A second barrier lies in the lack of trained teachers to teach GIS in schools. However, our experience here has been more encouraging. We have found that geography teachers are enthusiastic about re-skilling in this area and moreover we have found that training programs to bring them up to a level to teach elementary GIS do not need to be long. Indeed, a few days of intensive teaching with regular follow-ups over the Internet is all that is needed. There is then great scope for us to become the first State in Australia to be teaching SIS on a significant scale in our schools. If we are to gain an edge in having SIS as a major element in the State's economic development strategy, it is important that this opportunity is

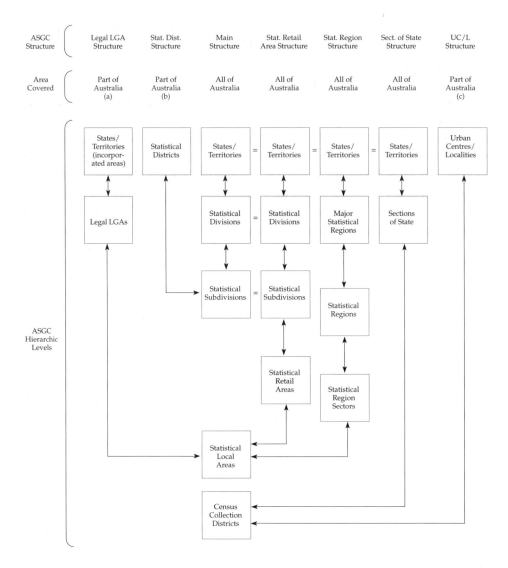

NOTES / SYMBOLS:
(a)   The incorporated part of Australia
(b)   The part of Australia covered by all Statistical Districts.
(c)   The part of Australia covered by all Urban Centres/Localities.
=     means equality between adjoining levels.
↔     means that the spatial units in adjoining hierarchic levels are related to each other by aggregation or disaggregation.

Figure 7. Australian Standard Geographical Classification (ASGC)

seized without delay. In the process it will provide a great opportunity for us to give the next generation of South Australians one tool at least to be more involved in the planning processes shaping their daily lives.

A final consideration is that if GIS is to be used as part of a strategy to empower local communities, we must find ways of getting GIS into the community. While 30.3 per cent of the Australian population had computers in the home in 1996, it

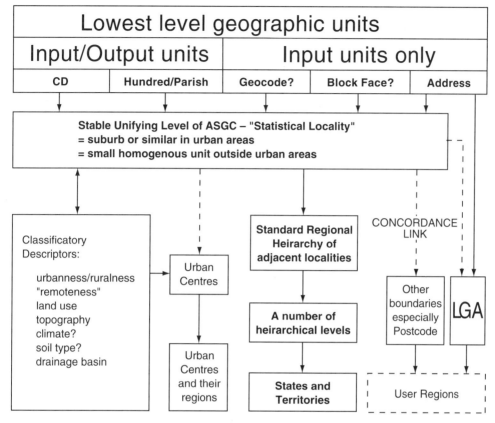

Figure 8. Overview of possible conceptual framework for a revised ASGC
Source: ABS 1997

is not realistic or equitable to rely on people gaining access to relevant GIS information about their community in their own homes. It is crucial that we develop highly user-friendly systems that provide such an opportunity in relevant public places. In particular, local public libraries are increasingly seen as local resource centres and part of this should involve access to GIS with relevant information about the local community. This type of thing can be done now if there is the political will to do so. We may even consider placing such systems in other public places such as local council chambers or even major shopping precincts.

## Conclusion

I have attempted in this article to keep my feet on the ground. So often discussions about information technology become flights of fantasy about how the world might be in some undetermined time in the future. I have attempted to demonstrate that while SIS technology and methodology is developing rapidly, what is already available has the capacity to assisting in the process of making social planning more people oriented. On the other hand, we have to be careful not to go overboard about the technology because that is all it is. It still has to be backed up by good social science if it is to be used effectively. SIS is a tool to help us do the things we have always done in a quicker and smarter way. This may mean us doing things more cheaply but it also can mean we can do things in a fairer way and take into consideration the needs of the whole community in developing policy and programs. As a social scientist and citizen I am concerned about the manifest growing inequality in Australian society. To arrest this trend and reverse it will take a massive effort of political will and significant economic and social change. We at the Key Centre believe that GIS has a small but nevertheless significant role to play in such an effort. It can do this, firstly, by assisting in policy and program development through the effective and timely analysis of the situation in communities and regions which place the people of those areas at the centre of attention. Secondly, it can be used to better inform communities about the policies, programs and processes impinging on their daily lives and hopefully help empower them to become actively involved in shaping those policies, programs and processes.

## Notes

1    H Scholten and M Van der Vlugt, 'A Review of Geographic Information Systems in Europe', in L Worrall (ed.) *Geographic Information Systems: Development and Applications* (Belhaven Press, London, 1990) pp. 13-40.

2    P Page, 'GIS and Social Sciences', *Geography, Organising Our World: Proceedings of the Thirteenth Annual ESRI Conference,* Vol.1, in (ESRI, Los Angeles 1993) pp. 385-396; G J Hugo, 'The Role of GIS in Solving Socio-Economic Problems Associated with Sustainable Settlement in Australia'. Paper presented at the Annual Conference of the Australasian Urban and Regional Information Systems Association Inc., (Adelaide, November 1993); G J Hugo, 'GIS and Socio-Economics', *GIS User,* (1994) No. 6, pp. 46-47; Worrall, (ed.) *Geographic Information Systems: Development and Applications;* D A Plane and P A Rogerson *The Geographical Analysis of Population with Applications to Planning and Business,* (John Wiley and Sons: US 1994); A Conning, 'The Use of Geographical Information Systems (GIS) in Demography', in International Union for the Scientific Study of Population, *International Population Conference: Montreal 1993,* Vol. 3, (Liege, International Union for the Scientific Study of Population 1993) pp. 169-174; H Coucelis, 'Geographically Informed Planning: Requirements for Planning Relevant GIS'. Paper presented to 36th North American Meeting of the Regional Science Association, Santa Barbara (1989).

3    Page 'GIS and Social Sciences', p. 386.

4    G J Hugo, 'What Population Studies can do for Business', *Journal of the Australian Population Association,* Vol. 8, No. 1, (1991) pp. 1-22.

5    Scholten and Van der Vlugt 'A Review of Geographic Information Systems in Europe' p. 28.

6    Conning 'The Use of Geographical Information Systems (GIS) in Demography' p. 171.

7    Scholten and Van der Vlugt 'A Review of Geographic Information Systems in Europe' p. 23.

8    E Ng and R Wilkins, 'How Far is it to the Nearest Hospital Facility in Canada? Calculating Distances Using Information Derived from Addresses and Postal Codes'. Paper submitted to Session 31, 'The Use of Geographical Information Systems in Demography', XXnd General Population Conference, International Union for the Scientific Study of Population (IUSSP), Montreal, Quebec, 24 August–1 September (1993).

9    L Rosero-Bixby, 'Physical Accessibility to Health Facilities in Costa Rica', in International Union for the Scientific Study of Population, *International Population Conference, Montreal,* 1993, pp. 185-190.

10   Page, 'GIS and Social Science' p. 390.

11   B J Gamer, 'GIS for Urban and Regional Planning and Analysis in Australia', in Worrall (ed.), *Geographic Information Systems: Development and Applications,* pp. 41-64.

12   L Worrall, 'Prospects and Challenges', in Worrall (ed.), *Geographic Information Systems: Development and Applications,* pp. 1-12; Coucelis 'Geographically Informed Planning: Requirements for Planning Relevant GIS'.

13   M Birkin, G P Clarke, M Clarke, and A G Wilson, 'Geographical Information Systems and Model-Based Locational Analysis: Ships in the Night or the Beginnings of a Relationship', *Working Papers,* School of Geography, Leeds University, No. 498 (1987).

14   B Badcock, *Background to the National Urban Indicators Project 1981-91-2001: Methodological and Technical Issues,* Working Paper, Key Centre for Social Applications of GIS, Adelaide (forthcoming).

15   C Maher, J Whitelaw, McAllister, R Francis, J Palmer, E Chee and P Taylor, *Mobility and Locational Disadvantage within Australian Cities,* (BIMPR and Department of Prime Minister and Cabinet: Canberra 1992).

16   A Beer, 'Roasting an Old Chestnut: Locational Disadvantage, Spatial Inequality and Government Policy', in *Locational Disadvantage and Spatial Inequality: New Perspectives on an Old Debate,* Proceedings of a Seminar, Geography Discipline, Flinders University of SA, (July 1994).

17   C A Forster, 'Restructuring and Residential Differentiation: Has Adelaide Become a More Unequal City?', *South Australian Geographical Journal,* Vol.91, pp. 46-60 (1991); C A Forster, Discussant's Comments: Locational Disadvantage, Outer Suburbia and Urban Myths, in *Locational Disadvantage and Spatial Inequality: New Perspectives on an Old Debate,* Proceedings of a Seminar, Geography Discipline, Flinders University of SA, (July 1994); F J B Stilwell, *Reshaping Australia: Urban Problems and Policies* (Pluto Press: Leichhardt 1993); Australian Institute of Family Studies, 'Inequality: 1986 to 1991', *Newsletter* accompanying A. Burbidge, *Families and Services: AIFS Working Paper No. 12,* (AIFS: Melbourne 1994); J Glover, and T Woollacott, *A Social Health Atlas of South Australia,* 2 Vols., ABS Catalogue No.4385.0 (Sunrise Press: Kent Town, 1992); DHHCW *Project Report of the Local Area Research Studies on Locational Disadvantage,* (Social Justice Strategy, Department of Health, Housing and Community Services: Canberra 1992); B Gregory and B Hunter, 'The Spatial Structure of the Labour Market, in Australian Urban and Regional Development Review', *Metropolitan Planning in Australia,* Workshop Papers #3, (Commonwealth of Australia: Canberra 1994); National Housing Strategy, *Australian Housing: The Demographic, Economic and Social Environment,* Issues Paper 1, (AGPS: Canberra 1992); Industry Commission *Taxation and Financial Policy Impacts on Urban Settlements, Vol.1 Report,* Report No.30, (AGPS: Canberra 1993); B A Badcock, 'Stressed-Out Communities': "Out-of-Sight, Out-of-Mind", *Urban Policy and Research,* Vol. 12, No. 3 (1994a); B A Badcock, 'Towards More Equitable Cities: A Receding Prospect?', in P.Troy (ed.), *Australian Cities,* (Cambridge University Press: Melbourne 1994b), pp. 165-184.

18   A Beer, A Bolam and A Maude, *Beyond the Capitals: Urban Growth in Regional Australia,* (AGPS: Canberra 1994).

19   R G Gregory and B Hunter, 'The Macro Economy and the Growth of Ghettos and Urban Poverty in Australia', *Discussion Paper No. 325,* (Centre for Economic Policy Research, Australian National University, April 1995); L S Bourne, 'Social Inequalities, Polarization and the Redistribution of Income Within Cities: A Canadian Example'. Paper presented at Small Area Indicators Workshop, National Key Centre for Social Applications of Geographical Information Systems, Adelaide, 23 April 1996.

20   C Kilmartin, 'Regional Disadvantage and Unemployment', *Family Matters,* No. 37, 1993 pp. 42-45; J Disney, 'Regional Development and Australia's Future'. Paper presented at the Annual Earle Page Lecture, University of New England, Armidale, 25 August 1992; Task Force on Regional Development, *Developing Australia: A Regional Perspective—A Report to the Federal Government,* 2 Vols., (AGPS, Canberra 1993); K Zagorski, 'Regional Differences in Economic Segmentation and SocioEconomic Achievement in Australia', *Research in Social Stratification and Mobility,* Vol. 9, 1990 pp. 217-249; Economic Planning Authority (EPAC), *Urban and Regional Trends and Issues,* Council Paper No. 46, AGPS: Canberra, 1991; Beer, Bolam and Maude, Beyond the Capitals: Urban Growth in Regional Australia; Bureau of Industry Economics, *Regional Development Patterns and Policy Implications,* (AGPS: Canberra 1994).

21   G J Hugo, 'Australia: The Spatial Concentration of the Turnaround', in A.G. Champion (ed.), *Counterurbanisation: The Changing Pace and Nature of Population Deconcentration,* (Edward Arnold: London 1989) pp. 62-82; G J Hugo, 'Locational Disadvantage: Development of a Data Model to Support Government Decision Making'. Report prepared for the Office of Geographic Data Co-ordination, Department of Premier and Cabinet, Victoria, (March 1995); P Smailes, 'Demographic Response to Rural Restructuring and Counterurbanisation in South Australia, 1981-1991, *International Journal of Population Geography,* Vol. 2, 1996 pp. 261-287 .

22   M Bell, K Nicolson, M Blake, and I McQueen, 'Forecasting Population Growth and Housing Development for Small Areas Using GIS'. Paper prepared for Informal Session 22, Remote Sensing and GIS for Data Collection and Analysis, 23rd General Population Conference, Beijing, China, 11-17 October 1997.

23   *Australian Financial Review,* 21 March 1997.

24   Department of Education and Community Services (DECS) *Mid Year Census 1996: Student Enrolment Data,* (DECS: Adelaide 1996).

25   Australian Bureau of Statistics, *Australian Standard Geographical Classification (ASGC) Review: Phase One Report,* (ABS: Canberra 1996); Australian Bureau of Statistics, *Australian Standard Geographical Classification (ASGC) Review: Phase Two Report,* (ABS: Canberra 1997).

*Deane Fergie*

# Australian Identity: Unsettled and Terrifying Representations

This article is about Australian culture, experience and representations. It is about the material consequences of representations in every day life. It asks questions about Australian culture by examining a variety of orientations to that central, interior, region of our cultural topography, defined by remaining beyond the settled districts: the 'outback'. It is based in ethnographic fieldwork, anthropology's key methodology which seeks to gain insights into culture by examining taken-for-granted assumptions and practice in the every day lives of others by engaging *with* them in their lives, typically for a period of a year or more.

This article emerges from about twelve months of ethnographic fieldwork from a base in the town of Marree, in which my husband Rod Lucas and I observed and participated in the lives of people in the Marree-Birdsville Track District—a region which many Australians might recognise, as I did well before I went there, as an exemplary region of the outback. This is a region with a history of complex identity: it is home to people who are identified as Aboriginal, Afghan and white or European Australians. My growing experience of life in that region, based in classic anthropological methodologies, required me to go beyond those methodologies and disciplinary strengths, and to explore that community's situatedness in time, space and broader cultural and political processes.

Over the course of that period of research I concluded that my analysis of the cultural lives of people in the Lake Eyre Basin must explore how metropolitan texts have shaped popular visions of our interiors, and how framing vistas have

---

Deane Fergie, PhD, Lecturer in Anthropology; one of nine lecturers named as 'Living Legends by the Students' Associations annual *Counter Calendar* 1996, awarded the Stephen Cole the Elder Prize for Excellence in Teaching in 1998. She is the author of 17 articles, book-chapters and conference-papers including: 'Those horrible "H"s (Hindmarsh and Heretic): high drama and popular representations of Anthropology' (Australian Anthropological Society Conference) 1996.

been contested and shifted over time. My fieldwork in the Lake Eyre Basin suggested that, despite such shifts and contestations, these distant metropolitan frames have governed important aspects of outback life. They have framed legislation. They have framed public policy and practice. They have framed public perception. They set important limits, and predicate particular strategies of accommodation and resistance.

I will argue 'the outback' is a cultural mirage, a vista bent and reified in the haze of distance and framed by the slowly shifting sands of representation and cultural imaginings.

But first, a disclaimer. While *my* account of Australian interiors is exploratory, it is not a charted account of exploration. This journey lacks the imperial direction, surveying and measurement usually associated with exploration. It does not seek to blaze a trail for possession and settlement. On the contrary, this is *mud map* which seeks to *unsettle*. Its lines are as propositional, re-positionable and orienting as are the contours of culture and of self which it explores. This article traces a personal journey.

So let me orient you to the problem this article homes in on. The scene is the main street of Marree—in South Australia's Far North. Opposite the now defunct railway station platform, the action focuses on a flag pole donated some months earlier by a local pastoralist for the town's bicentennial celebrations, and, I understand, to be a focus of future Anzac day marches. It was NAIDOC day—the day set aside in the national calendar as the National Aborigines and Islander Observance Day. NAIDOC Day[1] 1988 was a day of dramatic symbolism and action throughout Australia. In towns and cities across the nation Aboriginal people massed to demonstrate the unsettling ambiguity of state recognition in the year declared to celebrate a bicentenary of the European occupation of the continent. In the tiny outback town of Marree it was also a day of high drama. As I have heard the events recounted, an Aboriginal flag was raised on the flagpole early in the morning, without fanfare. A little while later someone hauled it down and replaced it with the Australian flag. Later the two flags were flown together—at first with the Australian flag uppermost, later with the ordering reversed. This battle to be on top continued throughout the day as the flags were raised and lowered and restrung in innovative combinations. This local incident was a focus of rancorous debate and bitterness in the town for many months after we moved to live there. Indeed Rod and I were to witness the flag pole being given police protection on NAIDOC day 1989.

Marree's flag-raising incident was a very local expression of what was, in retrospect, a more pervasive national unease. It re-appeared stridently in the debate which, six years later in 1994, followed Cathie Freeman's victorious and proud flagging of her dual heritage at the Commonwealth Games. It appeared again when she was informed by the 1996 Australia Olympic authorities that she could hold none other than the *national* flag in the Olympic arena, and so positioned the colours of her Aboriginality closer to both her soles—on specially-made running shoes. Most recently debate about the place of Aboriginal people in the nation has focussed on the High Court's Wik decision, and the emergence of the Howard government's Ten Point Plan. The plan, the government would have us be convinced, sets up a resolution for the 'uncertainty' which emerges between an alleged conflict of interest in leasehold land between Aboriginal people and pastoralists—a conflict of interest which is, I argue, in large part a consequence of the parameters and never-nevers of our cultural topography and the polemics of national politics, albeit stirred to a frenzy on this occasion by the particularities of the Queensland government's politics of administrative miss-adventure.

But let us return to Marree and the Birdsville Track. I saw it long before I went there. My first memory of it comes from the 'GP' room of Yarralumla Primary School in Canberra in the 1960s. Grey box pleated serge pushed my tie into an unfettered lump under my chin. The knots of my garters itched up my legs. Thirty-five or so small chairs lined in the room. An overwhelming smell of floor polish and school-strength disinfectant cleared our passages and entombed us in them. Lots of dishevelled lumps like me waited in the darkened room—itchy bums and impatient feet while Mrs Wetzel (or was it Mrs Curran?) looped and fed the film into the famished machine. Clattering and jumping into composure, a new vision finally tunnelled through the dark frontier of our impatience.

I have no doubt now that it was *The Back of Beyond*—an award winning film about Tom Kruse driving the mail from Marree to Birdsville in the fifties.[2] I reckon it was shown in other 'general purpose' rooms across the country for the next decade or so; some of my friends schooled in other places also recognise the memory. It gave us images to think with. Its sponsors, Shell, made a good investment, even though it was BP that got its logo across another set of images when Sir Donald Campbell flew his Bluebird over the not so distant dry salt bed of Lake Eyre ten years later.[3]

Seeing Tom Kruse's struggles again, in the dining room of Marree's Great Northern Hotel in 1987, I had an eerie sense of *deja vu*. Some scenes were intensely familiar—like the battle to get the heavy mail truck up and over the dunes. Up to its gunwales in sand. Digging out the wheels. Laying down sheets of iron, and hurtling up and over. Homestead deliveries. A woman on the radio. The old rain-maker. And Tom Kruse's eyes slit against the sandy wind but still looking up the Track. This time I was seeing it *in situ* at the inaugurating conference of the Lake Eyre Basin Project. I was there with an invitation to join the Project as anthropol-ogist, but before I had committed myself to do so. As for Tom, he had long since retired from the Birdsville mail run and moved to Quorn.

Rod's memory of that back-of-beyond screening is not dominated by distant nostalgia. His recall focuses vividly on the way Aboriginal viewers tapped his leg to name and locate the social identities of the film's other players. They gave names, relations and futures (now also past) to the ragamuffin kids clambering over the truck as it was loaded and chasing it out to the town gate. These viewers' interests were not with the heroism or struggles of the trip. Nor with the nature of the terrain. Rather, their viewing seemed to be framed by remembering and re-visiting people in their social world. Sandy the rainmaker was not an image. He was a relative. He had a biography, like all those who appeared, which transcended the film and was known to many local viewers.

One morning in that week of our first visit to Marree, Rod and I excused ourselves from the conference proceedings and drove along the Birdsville Track to the ruins of the mission at Killalpaninna. We had, only months before, returned from fieldwork on a lush tropical island off the north-east coast of Papua New Guinea. Could we work happily in such a different environment out here?

We sat in the sand somewhere near where John Heyer had filmed scenes in *The Back of Beyond* the year before I was born. The wind had blown the sand off coffins and old bones in the cemetery. Not much more than the footings of the old buildings now remained. The Lake Eyre Basin stretched all around us in its vastness. My childhood vistas of Australia, in which the outback was located, were beyond the horizon of my experience. They were largely confirmed in this adult encounter: framed as they were by newspaper and magazine reports, a stack of dog-eared Bony books, my schooling in a history of Australia framed by accounts of exploration, a geography of aridity whose contemporary hopes were the Murrumbidgee Irrigation and Snowy Mountains Hydro-Electricity Schemes, and in films and newsreels like this of the Back of Beyond. For me, then, the quintessential outback was an arid desert: vast, empty, desolate, a place of cruel beauty in which it was only too easy for humans or beasts to perish of thirst in the searing heat. Like many of my city-raised contemporaries my vistas of the outback were framed by an equation between the desolation and emptiness of the region's terrain and the social isolation and loneliness in which outback residents, I believed, battled the adversity of their environment. In this I was the inheritor of a shifting lineage of imaginings of Australia and its outback.

Popular texts would have it that the outback is timeless and unchanging. But as cultural terrain the sands have shifted dramatically over the past one hundred and seventy five years or so. Over the course of our fieldwork I came to see these ideas as cultural mirages.

In his book *Imagined Communities* Benedict Anderson reflected on the origin and spread of nationalism and proposed that a nation 'is an imagined political community—and imagined as both inherently limited and sovereign'. Anderson went on to suggest that 'nations are imagined communities because the members of even the smallest nation will never know most of their fellow-members, meet them, or even hear of them, yet in the minds of each lives the image of their communion … Communities are to be distinguished … by the style in which they are imagined'.[4]

Similarly I propose that the terrain of the nation is imagined—Australia is a cultural topography. This is not just a factor of the size of the continent we call Australia—so that we cannot know more than a small fraction of the nation's territory. There is another way in which Australia is profoundly imagined terrain. For the territory of Australia has a powerful and recognised history in the western imagination as well as our own. *Terra Australis* appeared on maps centuries before it was seen on the horizon by western sea-farers. This is, I suggest, a profound and enduring cornerstone of our national history. It has allowed Australians to imagine a long heritage in western history. Indeed in one of the earliest histories of Australia the first mapping of *Terra Australis* yet to be discovered, was attributed to Ptolemy's map from 150 AD. Another early history of Australia (particularly compelling for its apparent anticipation of the humour of Elle Mcfeast and Wogs at Work) claimed that Terra Australis was first heralded in an Ancient Greek myth starring a bloke called *Theopompous.* Certainly the idea of Terra Australis had taken solid and conspicuous form in the southern reaches of global cartography by the sixteenth century.

By claiming to be *Terra Australis* found, Australia asserts a long and auspicious history in the Western imagination. The continent the nation has settled upon is ancient. But the grounds that this nation has come to occupy were not knowable, as *Terra Australis* or Australia, before they were arrived upon by European explorers. *Terra Australis,* a posited great south land lacking particular shape and without parallel in either latitude or longitude, was imagined somehow to fill an absence on the globe. *Terra Australis* was a conceptual counter-balance to known realms. This continent, *as Australia,* was founded in the journeys, charts and accounts of explorers. Only on account of explorers' charts could Australia be arrived at and settled into. It was explorers who opened up a space in world history for this nation to occupy. It was they who impelled us on the process of filling that space with distinguishing features, of colonising the continent and defining it with European meanings.

The framing views of Australia's interiors have shifted from early visions of *a fertile inland sea* (see, e.g., Figure 1), to the many decades in which images of the region as Australia's *dead heart* have dominated popular imaginings. Now it is clear that the ensemble of ideas summed up in the idea of the dead heart is being contested by the vision I characterise as the *redemptive wilderness heartlands.* The idea of a fertile inland sea or great river had, it seems, a compelling cultural logic. Eurocentric geographic logic deduced from empirical observation that rivers ran into seas. So when, in 1817, explorers found that the Lachlan river ran *away* from the eastern seaboard the matter seemed settled. Expeditions were mounted to survey the expected blessing.

A passage from Charles Sturt (referring to his stranding at Depot Creek in 1844) provided evocative images, I argue, which were critical to the withering away of the idea of the interior harbouring a sea of fertility—though even as he wrote the words Sturt himself still harboured hopes of finding an inland sea. This passage,

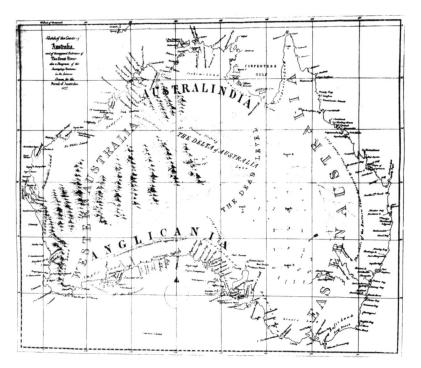

Figure 1. 'Friends of Australia', *Australians: A Historical Atlas*,
Fairfax, Syme and Weldon Associates, 1987

however, provided ghastly images in whose shadows a contesting view could begin to take form.

> the tremendous heat that prevailed had parched vegetation and drawn moisture from everything ... Under [its effect] every screw in our boxes had been drawn, and the horn handles of our instruments, as well as our combs, were split into fine laminae. The lead dropped out of our pencils, our signal rockets were entirely spoiled; our hair, as well as the wool on the sheep, ceased to grow, our nails had become as brittle as glass ... we found it difficult to write or draw, so rapidly did the fluid dry in our pens and brushes

The image of *a fertile inland sea* gradually perished in the desolating heat and vast aridity which made real-life explorers into parched corpses and led once-hopeful pastoralists to walk off the stations they had sought to establish in the interior.

By the mid 1860s new visions of the outback were emerging from the failed corporeality of explorers like Leichhardt and Burke and Wills. Visions of the continent mimicked their physicality. Its heart, like theirs in discovering it, was dead.

This monstrous and mortifying realisation made carrion of the idea that the continent had a fecund inland sea at its core. The 'sea' was a vast and empty expanse of life sapping salt. They gave it the honorary title of 'Lake'. Vivid imaginings of fertility were chased away by as extreme ideas of sterility and death.

Even when Europeans moved to take up residence in these regions they failed to convert this terrain into 'settled areas'. Their beasts only grazed the surface of the outback. Australia, it began to seem, had a *heart that was beyond redemption*. The outback was back of beyond—beyond taming, beyond cultivation. The outback was beyond life. The popular ascension of this ensemble of ideas after decades of contention between it and the vistas of a fertile inland sea became apparent by the time of the severe droughts of the 1890s.[5]

The ensemble of ideas and images that crystallise under the broad heading of the Dead Heart have persisted. They are typified by images of searing heat, red dust and vast, empty desolation. Social parallels of these ideas also persist. Desolation, isolation and loneliness are the inevitable consequences for non-Aboriginal people who seek to settle there. They must battle adversity. For this reason the Dead Heart made those who sought to settle it into heroes and heroines for a time. Those who ventured to make their lives in these perverse, unbridled lands were seen somehow as real Australians, real battlers, real characters in their loneliness and constant confrontation with desolation and death.

These ideas are the focus of a common genre of photography. Best accomplished with substantial depth of field and a wide angled lens held low and pointing up to the subject, this technique produces images of individuals or small groups appearing to stand in the midst of a vast nothingness. The horizon, far in

Figure 2. 'Loneliest Christmas' *Sunday Mail*, 24 December 1989

Figure 3. 'Loneliest Playground', *Advertiser,* December 1990.

the distance, dips away from them in the wide angle and disappears into that which cannot be seen, beyond the human subjects. In newspapers and magazines these images are captioned predicably. 'The loneliest Christmas' was the headline for a young outback mother photographed with her two young children which appeared in the Christmas Eve edition of the *Sunday Mail* in 1989. The next year a Birdsville Track girl was photographed riding her bike in a vast and empty landscape. That article was captioned 'The loneliest playground'.

By contrast, in this exotic schema the interior is understood as the natural niche for Aboriginal people. It is not their dead heart. It is not their never-never. It is 'ours'. They are conceived either to be destined to vanish into the desert sands or, by contrast with 'us', to be 'at home' in this interior. While it is remote from us, they are most vulnerable, most out of place and 'at sea' in the towns and cities which nurture our cultural existence.

Indeed, Aboriginal people are often defined, in effect, as part of or at one with the alien nature which defeats European culture. This racist perspective, which casts Aboriginal people and their culture as 'our' obverse, is also revealed and reinforced in the news, in popular literature, in film, and in important dimensions of everyday practice.

In January 1995, a report of journalist Peter Coster was headlined 'Clash of two worlds in old Marree'. It began:

> An image that I had long forgotten from childhood, that of a beautiful Aboriginal man and woman who go to their deaths torn between their tribal laws and those of the white man, returned to me in the desert of outback Australia.
>
> The Aborigines I saw in the intervening years were not beautiful but ruined by the clash of two cultures.
>
> The childhood image that I remembered was from the 1950 film *Jedda,* as

'Clash of Two Worlds' in Old Marree, *Sunday Mail*, January 1995

famous at the time as it is now forgotten.

As a child, I thought Robert Tudawali, as Marbuck and Ngarla Kunoth, as Jedda, were magnificent and doomed.

Those romantic thoughts are now tinged with reality, I think, as in the gibber desert we come upon an oasis. We are in a four-wheel drive which has crawled over the sand and stone, passing through the dog fence south of Marree, where the Oodnadatta and Birdsville tracks intersect.

The oasis is a mound spring, a source of bubbling life and energy to the Aborigines who have come here during their nomadic lives. In the four-wheel drive are three Aborigines who have brought me here.

Their spirits are lifted by the land and they are excitedly running towards the water, they throw off their clothes and sink into the spring.

One of the men is bearded, strikingly handsome and deep black like Robert Tudawali. He is changed from how I saw him earlier, slapping through the dust in thongs back in Marree.

This desert reality does not travel well. Aboriginal spirituality blooms in the bush but is dead in the city. It is as if there are two stories, one there and one here ...[6]

When I saw the article headlined 'Loneliest Christmas' in the *Sunday Mail* I was puzzled about where the horizon-bending photograph was posed. For Muloorina is a station whose elaboration of built structures have been compared with those of a small town.[7] Where, I wondered, had the photographer managed to find the clear space in which the mother and her children were framed as lonely figures in a vast and empty landscape? The answer was disarmingly simple. The photograph was taken on the 'homestead's' airstrip—its least 'built up' area.[8]

Similarly I discovered that the 'Loneliest Playground' of my young friend Jodie Oldfield was not the environs of her home: Mungerannie homestead. Rather the photographer had got her to ride down the Birdsville Track so that he could get the effect he wanted. The image of vast emptiness was a consequence of placement and positioning and headlining in each case. They were consequences of a larger cultural frame.

The character of the outback is being fought over once again. We are now in the midst of a period of contestation between the ensemble of images of the *dead heart* and alternative imaginings of a *redemptive wilderness heartland*. In this more recent vision the emphasis is on lifesaving and redemption rather than sterility and death. Dating perhaps from the publication of Patrick White's *Voss*[9] the new constellation is primarily a post-Roxby Downs phenomenon.[10]

Environmental images of the interior presently have two primary poles. The first focuses on the life-saving but fragile bio-diversity which remains in these areas. The other is concerned with the protection of the spiritual redemption that some feel this natural desert offers. As a consequence of 'green' activism some parts of the outback are now classified as 'wilderness'—valued officially for their 'naturalness and remoteness'.[11] In 1990 a discussion paper was publicly circulated in the run-up to the establishment of a *Wilderness Protection Act* in South Australia.[12] That paper defined 'wilderness quality' as 'the extent to which land is remote from and undisturbed by the influences and impacts of modern techno-logical society'.[13] The definition was refined in respect of Aboriginal people:

> The definition identifies the impacts of 'modern society' as affecting remote-ness and naturalness. The definition acknowledges that *Aboriginal traditional land use is a part of the wilderness we wish to preserve* (emphasis mine).[14]

This new vista on our cultural horizon is not, though, the radical departure it first appears. Rather it is, I suggest, a new versions of the 'incompatible worlds' perspective. It makes Aboriginal people 'wild'. It transforms their white neigh-bours into displaced persons.

Things do not always disappear into the desert sand. Sometimes they emerge from them. In Vaseline Intensive Care's 'Skin Science Update' safari-suited swim-ming star Lisa Forrest walks towards the camera in a vast, wide-angled outback landscape.

> Out here in Sturt's Stony Desert the temperature reaches up to 55 degrees. Yet it's under this scorching heat that grows the very thing that will help soothe sunburn. It's called aloe vera … Research shows Vaseline Intensive Care with Aloe soothes the drying effects of sunburn. Sometimes the best scientific dis-coveries come from nature.
> From intensive research comes Vaseline Intensive Care.

This advertisement demonstrates the rejuvenating, nurturing capacities of a 'natural science' by juxtaposing it with the threat of dehydration which stopped Sturt, almost dead in his tracks.

The striking feature of our dominating images of the outback over time—ensembles of ideas as contrasting as a fertile inland sea, dead heart, and redemp-tive wilderness heartlands—is that these are distant metropolitan images. Children brought up along the tracks don't generally ride along them.

In 1989, after a number of shorter trips, Rod and I had moved into a govern-ment house in Marree's First Street and spent the good part of that year there. On a number of shorter field trips between 1988 and 1991 we singly or together stayed in town or up the track in our tent, a swag, or in the hospitality of new-found friends' homes. When not engaging in everyday life, like ethnographers around the world, we took photos, recorded genealogies and memories and the stories which emerged from them, of the vitality of life in this place. What was clear almost immediately, was that this was a community with an intense and extensive social life.

As a resident I went to 'Ladies lunches' in the pub, the most flamboyant of which focussed on a far-off Melbourne Cup but included a hat competition for the ladies and a local foot race where the runners were auctioned off before they raced, and where the winner's ironic trophy was a caricature of the back end of a horse. Rod and I went to the many of the huge parties that are a feature of sociality in this place to mark comings-of-age, significant birthdays, wedding anniversaries, christenings, engagements, homecomings, farewells, and those which were part of public events like the Picnic Races. We went to school picnics, gymkhanas, bronco branding, other horse sports events, as well as NAIDOC Day celebrations. We went to cabarets, and to balls and blue light discos. We stood with others, drinks and food often in hand, around railway sleepers burning in forty-four gallon drums, at parties opposite Deano's Casino in Ghan town, at the Caravan Park, at the back of the Arabanna Centre. And we went to special events like Motorkhana's and Bingo nights, a bicycle ride in aid of the Flying Doctor from Etadunna to Marree and the 'Birdsville Track Splash' an event held to celebrate the water of the usually dry Cooper's Creek crossing the Birdsville Track in 1989. I bought more raffle tickets in a month living in Marree than I had bought in all my life before I moved there.

With a VHF radio I was also able to participate in the intense life of talk-back radio, in which everyone within earshot was privy to the conversations of all others. I was party to meetings held on the radio. I too used it to keep in touch with my friends and to conduct business.

This was no locus of loneliness. Rather it was a place in which, if you weren't careful you could get social burnout. If solitude was possible, it seemed to me that it was only possible through clear choice and deliberate manoeuvring.

Local politics was no less vital and exhausting. We were privy to battles for succession to property and status. We observed the intensity, nuances and agendas of local politics. We came to recognise how selves are presented and changed in all manner of contexts by locals. And we came to realise how contentious is the term 'local', and the symbolic values of its use.[15]

We were not locals. We were a unique kind of 'breeze through'—a category used to refer to temporary residents, particularly the kind who stick their noses in where they aren't always welcome. Even so we joined a number of local committees and slugged it out. At one stage I estimated that there was one committee for every ten people (of any age) resident in the District. I remember sitting talking to a neighbour on her fence in Marree when a small bunch of tourists walked past. One of their number asked 'What on earth do you people do here?' My neighbour responded laconically 'Ah, we get along'. Then as they got out of earshot she added 'I didn't want to tell her I was on my way to my third meeting of the day!'

For 'locals' this is not a sparse landscape devoid of differentiation and meaning. It is brim full of significance and meaning. A drive along the Birdsville Track is not impartial or undifferentiated. It is not just bore-heads and homesteads that map out the journey along the track. Grids, trees, tanks, yards, areas in need of road repair and even stock, locate people in time, place and relationships. 'Big Red' is a sandhill used for rugga bugga tourist sport just outside of Birdsville. It is, I think, one of the few names of sandhills known by tourists. By contrast 'Jack's tank' is off the main tourist track. It is a landmark in time and space for people who work and live in that stretch of country. Jack may now be long gone but his name, and the water it locates, signposts significance.

The ethnography developed in unexpected directions. Our fieldwork coincided with a boom time for expeditionary tourism. Sometimes we would marvel at the proportion of Australia's GDP parked outside the Great Northern. At the same time our fieldwork home became a staging post for many 'scientific' expeditions. So we joined a number of them as ethnographers and served expeditionary tourists at service outlets in town and up the track. We observed the popularity of unmarked photographic posts whose only attraction seemed to be the view that their rises gave of an apparently vast and empty landscape. We heard these ideas spoken by visitors struck by the apparent emptiness, and barrenness of the environment—even after rain when the swales were filled with bright flowers. We watched expeditioners pitch camp and organise their 'suburban' quarters. On one all-women expedition I watched as clusters of tents, erstwhile specialist science groups, became small canvas settlements named Vaucluse and Footrot Flats. Recently in a book on how to travel in outback Australia on a budget, I read an admission by its author which resonates with my own observations of outback tourists. He wrote:

> When I search my photos showing that it can be freezing cold in Alice Springs or pouring with rain in the Simpson Desert, they aren't there ... but there are dozens showing wheel-ruts over sand-dunes or dust swirling over red dirt roads. Then I realise that I am as guilty as anyone of perpetuating the myths of the Outback—I have photo albums full of them.[16]

Local people enlivened the landscape for us. They revealed it to us as eminently cultural terrain. They uttered and pointed us to a cacophony of significances in the topography of their everyday lives. Gradually I came to realise the depth of their love for the country and the ties which bind them to it. When we first arrived we were several times regaled with the idea that 'This country gets into your blood' and of the people who came for a week, but never left. The country gets into your blood, I heard, by drinking bore water, by the dust getting into the

crevices of your skin and up your nose. One dimension of the process was manifest in the bands of hats: red dust impregnates the fabric of hats and is held there
by sweat. No question about it—there was something visceral in the way in which
many local people loved this country. As one pastoral patriarch told us: 'I know
every tree, every stone on this place.' I have no doubt that he does, even though
'this place' of his covers nearly two thousand square kilometres. Nor have I any
doubt about the intense depth of feeling he has for it or indeed that 'this place'
where he has lived for more than sixty years, means *everything* to him. Though his
is one of the smaller pastoral stations in the region, this is not an unusual level of
knowledge, or attachment. Another pastoralist, in a room decorated with framed
colour photographs of cattle, told me how he sometimes feels close to tears when
his prize bullocks are loaded up to be trucked to market. These beasts embody his
work of sweat and management, and what I have heard described as, the 'sweet-
ness' of this country. That that pastoralist and his sweet country grow beautiful
bullocks was framed all around his lounge room.

In 1993 Reg Dodd, prominent Marree resident, photographer and chairman of
the Marree Arabanna People's Committee, held a joint Adelaide exhibition with
painter Malcolm McKinnon. They called their exhibition 'Behind the Picture:
Explained Landscapes'. Reg Dodd explained:

> Tourists come through this place and say that there's nothing to see out there.
> They say it's a big country with nothing in it. But I can go out and photo-
> graph any number of things just in a tiny area. I take photographs of things
> in their natural habitat. Nearly all my photos are of this area because I can
> identify with the places and the images: they're a part of me. The photos
> explain what I know about the place, share my experience ...[17]

Not long after we arrived to take up residence in Marree we drove an Aboriginal
elder along the Birdsville Track. As I drove along she pointed to hills, and lakes,
and other features in the landscape and located them in a system of meaning
which took other tracks as their points of departure, and embodied other signifi-
cations of boundary and distinction. She made connections between this cultural
topography, human beings and its other inhabitants. She sang the country. At
other times we saw how pastoralism and stock work gave identity to both
Aboriginal and non-Aboriginal people. How they are unbridled by a heritage they
share, while bound into the absurdities of flag-raising incidents and all the contestation and bitterness such moments signal.

The years of our fieldwork, at the end of the eighties, and beginning of the
nineties coincided with a period of Labor government in South Australia and the
reform and initiation of a swag of legislation affecting the life and work of pastoralists. This was also a period during which pastoralists felt themselves to be
under siege, and their livelihood and way of life threatened by an important shift
in public perception. The country they grazed was asserted to be fragile. One
pastoralist said of this, 'What's this fragile business, Deane? This country's a strong

bugger'. Pastoralists also recognised that their status as national heroes was being shifted, as a consequence of an environmental campaign, to that of heinous destroyers.

In this period the Pastoral Act was redrafted and renamed the Pastoral Land Management and Conservation Act. It was the centrepiece of a new ensemble of legislation governing life on the inland pastoral stations: A Soil Conservation and Land Care Act, Native Vegetation Management Act, Water Resources Act and the Wilderness Protection Act. But from a pastoral perspective, worse was to come. On the eve of the 1993 Federal election, Paul Keating made the following announcement as part of his party's environmental platform, out of the blue:

> Today I am pleased to announce that the South Australian Government has agreed to work with the Commonwealth to assess the environmental values of the magnificent and unique Lake Eyre region for World Heritage listing ... this will represent a major step onward for the conservation of our fragile arid regions.[18]

Pastoralists fought back, modelling their campaign on techniques they had seen used against them by environmental campaigners, and using political skills honed in their campaign to influence the new State legislation. As their advertising shows, they appealed to metropolitan Australia by using visual images associated with the dead heart. In the end, they won.

But with the election of the Federal Coalition government in 1996 the heat has gone off inland pastoralists, and instead been turned up on Aboriginal people. Legislative revision of Aboriginal people's rights and heritage is now taking place—proposed amendments to the Aboriginal and Torres Strait Islander Protection Act at the Federal level, and at the State level the Aboriginal Heritage Bill are on the table. ATSIC is under threat. Native Title is being doused. After a history of the denial by Australians and the nation-state of their occupation of their land and basic human rights, even to their children, the euphoria of Mabo is gone. Frustration, anguish and anger are growing. The rights in country acknowledged at last in the High Court's Mabo decision, and brought into law in the Native Title Act, are set to be thoroughly doused, if not extinguished, as the Prime Minister's Ten Point Plan becomes the basis for legislative amendment. The legal rights of Aboriginal people are clearly being backed into a corner in an apparent war of attrition between the interests of pastoralists and Aboriginal people.

But whose battle is it really? The recent swing against the interests and rights of Aboriginal people under Liberal and Coalition governments has clear parallels with that faced by pastoralists under Labor governments. What are the long term consequences of this oscillating and retributive pendulum of party polemic whose fulcrum is metropolitan stereotypes? I want to end this article by unsettling the polemics and suggesting that Aboriginal people and pastoralists share a great deal in their everyday lives.

Aboriginal people and pastoralists share a deep emotional and practical attachment to the land, albeit differently founded in their cultures. Aboriginal people feel themselves to be *of the land,* to be integral actors in its enduring cultural shaping and significances and diminished by distance from their land. Country is *in them.* The country *gets into* non-Aboriginal people. Pastoralists understand their relationship as one in which the country they live and work on gets into their pores, under their skin, and into their blood. Aboriginal people and pastoralists have *long shared* a mismatch between the depth of their attachments to the land and their legal rights in it. They share a long history of having their lives governed by metropolitan stereotypes.

In Wik the High Court decided, wisely in my view, that the rights of native title holders and pastoralists could coexist on pastoral leases. It determined that the interests of pastoralists would prevail if they were in conflict. In South Australia, as historian Rob Foster has demonstrated, pastoralism has always coexisted with the rights of Aboriginal people to use their land for traditional purposes.[19]

But what does any of this matter? What does it matter that there is a mismatch between the affective ties of both pastoralists and Aborigines in country and their rights in it. What does it matter that our national politics plays one group off against the other in the pendulum swings between Labor and Coalition?

In his recent book *Exploring Confrontation: Sri Lanka: Politics, Culture and History,* anthropologist Michael Roberts writes poignantly about how, in the early 1970s, he tried to organise a conference on 'the Sinhala:Tamil problem' in his homeland Sri Lanka. A colleague retorted then that 'There is no Sinhala:Tamil problem.' Roberts persisted: 'I was fully convinced that [this] assessment was erroneous— dangerously so. He, and others like him, were sitting on several time-bombs and quite oblivious to it. As the 1970s rolled by, this complacency remained—though the signs of Tamil discontent and impending dangers grew apace'.[20] Alas, Michael Roberts' fears were well-founded. Retributive conflict and violence is now a fundamental feature of Sri Lankan life. As we have come to see in Ireland, the Balkans, on the West Bank, in violent pockets around our globe, there seems no end to the bitterness of retributive violence. We might well ponder whether Australia is indeed, as I suspect we have long held, quarantined from the force of such retributive moral and affective logics.

The Australian outback is a cultural mirage: evanescent, oscillating, shimmering, never quite settled upon, this mirage provides a locating and identifying horizon for Australians from Bondi to Burnie, Broome and back. If the continent over which the first settlers asserted sovereignty was understood by them as unsettled, two hundred and more years later it is the outback, defined by remaining beyond the settled districts, which is an unsettling force at the heart of the nation.

### Acknowledgments

Andrew Hall of the *Advertiser* for permission to use material from the *Advertiser* and the *Sunday Mail*; G Nowell, photographer from the *Advertiser*; Neon Martin, photographer from the *Sunday Mail*

## Notes

1    The day of celebration declared by the National Aboriginal and Islander Day Committee

2    Made by John Heyer in 1954

3    See, for example, John Pearson, *Bluebird and the Dead Lake: The Story of Donald Campbell's Land Speed Record at Lake Eyre in 1964* (Collins: London, 1965)

4    Benedict Anderson, *Imagined Communities: Reflections on the Origin and Spread of Nationalism* (Verso: London, 1983) p. 6

5    J W Gregory, *The Dead Heart of Australia: A Journey around Lake Eyre in the summer of 1901-1902, with some account of the Lake Eyre Basin and the Flowry Wells of Central Australia* (John Murray: London, 1906)

6    Peter Coster, 'Clash of two worlds in old Marree', *Sunday Mail*, 5 March 1995, pp. 22-3. Published also the week before in Melbourne by the *Herald Sun*

7    See Roma Dalhunty, *The Spell of Lake Eyre*, (Lowden Publishing Co., Kilmore 1975) p. 62

8    Ironically the story belied the message of the photograph and 'Loneliest Christmas' headline. Fifty guests were expected that Christmas day for Christmas dinner at Muloorina

9    Patrick White, *Voss*, (Penguin Books: Harmondsworth, 1974)

10   It was the anti-uranium mining blockades at Roxby Downs in the early 1980s which seemed irretrievably to broaden the horizons of environmentalists from the littoral green belt (which until then firmly held their gaze) to Australia's arid centre. A crucial documentation of this shift in gaze can be found in the Australian Conservation Foundation mind-set breaking report 'What Future for Australia's Arid Lands?' Published in 1983

11   See R Leslie, D. Taylor and M. Maslen, *National Wilderness Inventory Handbook* (Australian Government Publishing Service, Canberra 1993)

12   Significant parts of the Lake Eyre Basin were targeted at an early stage for Wilderness Listing

13   Interim Wilderness Committee, Department of Environment and Planning, 'Discussion Paper for the proposed Wilderness Protection Act', December 1990, p. 8

14   ibid. p. 1

15   See, for example, Rod Lucas and Deane Fergie, 'A Nobbler at Blazes Well: The Policing of Alcohol in the Marree-Birdsville Track District', *Journal of the Historical Society of South Australia*, 1996, no. 24 pp. 28-45

16   Brian Sheedy, *Brian Sheedy's Outback Australia on a Budget* (Viking O'Neil, Ringwood 1987, 1990) p. 31

17   In exhibition notes for 'Behind the Picture: Explained Landscapes'. An exhibition of photographs by Reg Dodd and paintings by Malcolm McKinnon. Tandanya National Aboriginal Cultural Institute, Adelaide, September 1991

18   'Maintaining our Natural Advantage', environmental platform speech, 9 March 1993, p. 5

19   Robert Foster, 'The Origin of the Protection of Aboriginal Rights in South Australian Pastoral Leases', *Land, Rights, Laws: Issues of Native Title*, no. 24, August 1998.

20   Michael Roberts, *Exploring Confrontation: Sri Lanka: Politics, Culture and History* (Harwood: Switzerland, 1994) pp. 21, 23

*Philip Butterss*

# From Ned Kelly to
# Queens in the Desert

I want to begin this brief survey of some of the key films dealing with Australian masculinity by considering an excerpt from what is arguably the world's first feature film. There are only a few fragments, almost all that survives from *The Story of the Kelly Gang* directed by Charles Tait, and first screened in Melbourne on Boxing Day, 1906. Unlike later silent cinema, *The Story of the Kelly Gang* didn't use inter-titles to clarify what was going on; instead it relied on a lecturer and actors hiding behind the screen to explain the action and to provide the voices.[1]

Today, the model of frontier masculinity embodied by Ned Kelly is, like such fragments, fading and fragmentary. But for a long time, of course, it was a dominant image of manhood in Australian cinema and Australian culture, although by no means the *only* one. And it still remains as a ghostly presence in films that define their representation of Australian identity or Australian masculinity in relation to that tradition. But it may be true that even in 1906, this representation of masculinity contained some recognition of its own instability. Perhaps the audience's awareness of the actors behind the screen may have pointed to the performative nature of masculinity. Certainly, on the screen the cast iron costume is not sufficient to prevent this emblem of frontier masculinity having the legs shot out from underneath him.

*The Story of the Kelly Gang* was the first of a series of bushranging films which were the staple of the fledgling Australian film industry, and it was quickly followed by fourteen more such films (including the first *Robbery Under Arms*) dealing with a variety of historical and fictional figures. The flourishing genre came to

Philip Butterss, PhD, Lecturer in English Literature and Australian Studies, winner of the Irish Government Bicentennial Scholarship 1987-8. He is the editor of *Crossing Lines: Formations of Australian Culture* (ASAL) 1996, with C. Guerin and A. Nettelbeck; *Southwords: Essays on South Australian Writing* (Wakefield Press) 1995; and *The Penguin Book of Australian Ballads* (Penguin) 1993, with E. Webby.

*The Story of the Kelly Gang,* 1906

an abrupt halt in 1912 when the New South Wales government banned bush-ranging films.[2] Of course, the ban did not stop the production of such films permanently—there have been a further three versions of *Robbery Under Arms*, and at least five others about Ned Kelly. Nor did it put an end to the model of masculinity which these films valorised, a masculinity embodying the range of characteristics set out by Russel Ward in *The Australian Legend*, of which perhaps the most important were anti-authoritarianism, egalitarianism, and mateship. Other varieties of bushmen and pioneers were celebrated; war films such as Charles Chauvel's *Forty Thousand Horsemen* were often ripping yarns about bush-men battling a human enemy abroad, rather than a harsh landscape at home; and the urban larrikin is, in many respects, the bushman's city cousin, with similar connotations of 'non-conformism, irreverence and impudence'.[3]

In his book *Masculinities,* sociologist Bob Connell points to the importance of the creation of global empires in the construction of masculinity as we know it, arguing that the men who applied force at the colonial frontier were perhaps the first group to become defined as a masculine cultural type in the modern sense.[4] He also suggests that as religious legitimations for men's dominant position in Western culture have declined, there has been a rise in the importance of exem-plary masculinities—high profile individual examples of masculinity as can be found in the pulp western, the thriller, the sports broadcast and the Hollywood movie.[5] Exemplars of masculinity, whether legendary or real, have often been men of the frontier—Davy Crockett and John Wayne in the United States, for instance. In Australia, of course, the bush has been particularly prominent as a source for models of masculinity which privilege male power.

But from relatively early in the history of Australian cinema, movie-goers were *also* offered a much more ambivalent view of Australian masculinity in a series of films with their origins in Steele Rudd's stories of poor selectors. Films about the Hayseed family, and later the Rudd family itself, trod a fine line, managing to treat rural men as idiotic bumpkins while also endorsing the pioneer myth of brave struggle against a harsh land.

In the late 1990s it is easy to regard ourselves as enlightened, and to look back somewhat smugly, but, in fact, the early Australian cinema could sometimes allow men a much wider emotional range than most contemporary films do. Raymond Longford's 1919 version of *The Sentimental Bloke* presents its hero struggling to choose between the two models of masculinity identified by Marilyn Lake in her study of the 1890s 'masculinist' manhood and 'domestic man'.[6] Bill, the bloke, begins by living out a masculinist lifestyle, drinking to excess, gambling and fighting; but we also see him declaring his love for his Doreen, both privately and publicly, crying with remorse for not valuing her as highly as he should, and the film finishes with him gazing lovingly at his wife and new son, and vowing to work hard for his family. Sentimentality wins out over blokedom; adult manhood is finally equated with being a good husband and a good father.

### The revival

Although the Australian film industry flourished initially, the period from 1930 until 1970 was largely one of survival, in spite of the fact that Charles Chauvel was making his greatest films during these years. With the foundation of the Australian Film Development Corporation (AFDC) in 1970 there began a substantial revival in local cinema. One of the major goals of the AFDC and the various other funding bodies established during the 1970s and 1980s was to encourage film that represented Australia to Australians. Given the importance of male figures as images of Australian identity, examinations of *national* character have often also been examinations of *masculine* character, although not always consciously so.

In the first half of the twentieth century it might have been possible to assert an Australian identity that was homogenous and masculine, but particularly since the beginning of the film revival there have been considerable pressures on unified notions of both national and masculine identity. The increasing awareness of the multicultural nature of Australian society has made possible a conception of Australianness that foregrounds difference not sameness. And among the pressures on traditional ideas of an 'essential' and unitary masculinity have been the increasing prominence of gay men, indigenous men, and men from non-English speaking backgrounds in the public sphere; changes in the work patterns of Australian women; the influence of feminism in many areas of Australian culture; and perhaps even the rise of men's studies as an academic area.

As well as the kind of masculinity which operates to maintain men's dominant position in the culture—called hegemonic masculinity, by Connell—there is an increasing recognition of other kinds of masculinities, other ways of being a man, for example subordinated masculinities such as those lived by homosexual men, or masculinities marginalised from mainstream power by race or class. Much of the cinema since 1970 needs to be seen in the context of this breakdown in images of the monocultural nation, and in conceptions of a single, unified masculinity.

The film which, according to Graeme Turner, 'proved to be the catalyst' for the revival of the Australian film industry was *The Adventures of Barry McKenzie*,[7] but it was only one of a series of ocker films which were successful in the early and mid 1970s, like *Stork, Petersen* and the Alvin Purple films. The ockers featured here were easily identifiable as descendants of earlier larrikins, and, in many ways, were city cousins of the bushman—anti-authoritarian, egalitarian, and, in Bazza's case, wearing the same hat.

I saw *The Adventures of Barry McKenzie* for the first time recently and it was not at all the film I had expected from the clips I had seen, and from the way people talk about it. I expected a brash and aggressive assertion of a larrikin Australian identity—and certainly those elements were there—but I was not prepared for the prominence of the anxieties the film revealed both about Australian culture and Australian masculinity. From the opening title sequence, where the film announces that it has been classified by the Australian censor as NPA—No Poofters Allowed—it is clear that it is riddled with insecurities about Australian masculinity. Bazza is a virgin, but lies about his sexual exploits; stars in an advertisement for 'High Camp' cigarettes; and fails dismally as an Australian version of the Marlboro Man. Throughout the film, the audience is well aware of the fact that Barry Humphries is playing Bazza's aunt. And Bazza, himself, even has a moment of cross-dressing when—to prove to the police that the women's clothes in his Qantas bag are not his because they don't fit—he puts them on, only to find that they fit him like a glove.

*The Adventures of Barry McKenzie* is also interested in depicting Australian mateship. In one scene, Bazza has been dragged along to a young Tories dance, but is delighted to find an all-male group of Australians out the back. Allan Thomas points out that

> Barry's pleasure at finding his compatriots is evident, as is theirs at finding him. He abandons the dance and the young girl he arrived with, and joins in the fun. This largely takes the form of the consumption of large amounts of Fosters, preceded by shaking the cans, cracking them open and spraying the resultant foam over as many of the surrounding men as possible.[8]

Thomas argues that 'the ejaculatory quality of the boy's beer cans as they open them ... suggests the alternative that is so clearly present and so strongly repressed in the mythology of mateship'.[9]

Whether or not this is the case here, the possibility of an erotic element beneath the homosocial bond of mateship—and the repression of that element— is frequently apparent in films of the revival dealing with the relations between Australian men. It is there in *Gallipoli* in the loving looks exchanged between Archie and Frank; it is there as a possible undercurrent in the bond between Hando and Davey, the skinheads in *Romper Stomper,* and it is there in the relationship between the characters played by Hugo Weaving and Russell Crowe in *Proof*. At the beginning of *The Big Steal*, a film from 1990, one of Danny Clark's mates tries to convince the Claudia Karvan character to go out on a date with Danny. 'Danny Clark', she says, 'Why would I want to go out with him?' The mate replies 'He's one of the most interesting people I know'. She replies, sensibly, 'So why don't *you* go out with him?' In films about growing up, homosexuality is frequently raised as a threatening possibility, which is then carefully resolved. Commenting on the lack of substantial parts for women in films more generally, one critic has suggested that the main narrative function of the female lead is to prove that the male lead is not gay.

Many other films during the 1970s responded to the pressures on homogenous notions of Australianness and unitary notions of masculinity by depicting the conflict between groups of mates and 'others', against whom they defined their identify. As Meaghan Morris has noted, this careful delineation of group boundaries can be seen

> in the strenuously competitive, all-male working world of Ken Hannam's *Sunday Too Far Away* when one of the shearers, Sean Scully, writes to his wife and finds himself treated as a queer. Difference can also provoke complacent hilarity: the boys in *The FJ Holden* have their harmless fun terrorizing a 'wog' in his car.... Participation in a ritual of this kind is very much the pleasure offered by films like *Stork, Alvin Purple, Barry McKenzie, Petersen.*[10]

These films take varying perspectives on the kind of masculinity they portray, ranging from celebration to critique, but none were as powerfully condemning as *Wake in Fright*'s depiction of a 'distinctive blend of repression, violence and segregation' which it saw as 'one of the conditions of sexuality in Australian society'.[11]

The period films of the late 1970s and early 1980s were another site where the problematisation of Australian masculinity was played out, again in a variety of ways. *Gallipoli*—like *Sunday Too Far Away*, a few years earlier—was a nostalgic and sympathetic depiction of frontier masculinity and the mateship bond, but, at the same time, a eulogy which acknowledged the passing away of this kind of masculinity and bonding. *Gallipoli's* stunning final frozen image of the bullet wounds like Anzac medals on Archie's chest embodies a nostalgia for the passing of the bushman, and a recognition that he is to be succeeded by Frank, 'a sharp city lad' embodying a new image of an urban masculinity for the future.[12] But, in spite of the eulogies, frontier masculinity returned as a revenant in the biggest box office successes of the late 1970s and early-to mid-80s—the *Mad Max* cycle, *The Man from Snowy River,* and *Crocodile Dundee.*

*Mad Max* is a merging of a masculinity based on what would today be called risk-taking behaviour—reeking of petrol and testosterone—with frontier masculinity, this time set in a post-apocalyptic, but not too distant, future. In a history of Australian film shown on television in 1997, George Miller said that the Mad Max figure was interpreted as an outlaw samurai in Japan, a lone Viking in Scandinavia, and a gunslinger on wheels in the United States. In Australia he's at least in part the reckless Ned Kelly, with horse swapped for high-powered car.

It is a deeply contradictory vision, with Max 'forced' by circumstances and manipulation into becoming the hero that, we are told, society needs. That hero, however, is shown to be a socially dysfunctional individual, and ultimately to be as psychopathic as the Toecutter and the other misfits who are his quarry. This potentially dangerous side to the masculine hero has been explored much more often in the avenging gunslinger of American films about frontier masculinity.[13] And Mel Gibson's character in the *Lethal Weapon* films covers similar terrain.

Drawing on Judith Butler's work on gender as performance, Yvonne Tasker has argued that in Hollywood action films, the excessive bodies of characters such as Sylvester Stallone and Arnold Schwarzenegger are an instance of what she calls 'performing the masculine'. The extraordinary muscularity of these figures, operates as a signifier of masculinity, but at the same times undermines masculinity by presenting it as another form of costume, a performance. In a related way, in the *Mad Max* films, the hero's excesses also operate to question the very model of masculinity he represents.[14] (Thomas has argued this about Crocodile Dundee.)

One way to deal with contemporary pressures—in this case on traditional ideas of what it is to be Australian and what it is to be a man—is to escape into the past, and this was, of course, the strategy employed in *The Man from Snowy River.* It was perhaps *because* the kind of masculinity featured in this film could no longer have any direct connection to life in the 1980s that it received one of its fullest and most romanticised depictions. The lad from Snowy River masters the bush horses, masters the landscape, and masters the love interest played by Sigrid Thornton who, as Rose Lucas points out, is virtually indistinguishable from Bess, the missing horse.[15]

Lucas also suggests that the desire to appeal to an American market may have resulted in a more individualist focus—a shift from the egalitarian ethos at the heart of mateship.[16] But it is also true that mateship as an ideal has always had an uneasy co-existence with competition *between* men. In the ballad on which the film is based, the tension between individual and collectivity is already present, and the lad only becomes a 'man' when he leaves the others and charges off down the mountainside on his own. This individual (and competitive) act is a rite of passage which then allows him to return to the masculine fraternity as a full member.

*The Man from Snowy River* was the biggest box office success for an Australian film, but its returns were to be eclipsed by *Crocodile Dundee* a film which brought frontier masculinity into the 1980s. Paul Hogan has commented on the debt the Mick Dundee figure owes to the Australian masculine tradition, if in a back-handed way. He told London's *Time Out*:

> The character is an attempt to give Australia a hero. It's a country desperately short of heroes. We haven't got a Daniel Boone or a Robin Hood. All we ever had was Ned Kelly, an Irishman with a bucket over his head who pulled a few unsuccessful robberies a long time ago.[17]

In the first half of *Crocodile Dundee*, Mick has tamed the outback. In the second half of the film he tames an urban American landscape, conquering escalators, bidets, transvestites, uppity women, and racial threats. Mick Dundee lives out the frontier model of masculinity, but there is also an element of self-deprecation in the weak imitation of Tarzan.[18] Hogan is aware that it is difficult to take that kind of masculinity seriously any more, but by acknowledging that difficulty in half-laughing at the absurdity of it all, it becomes possible for the film to produce a full-blown and affectionate, if somewhat parodic, representation of this stock figure.

## Aboriginal masculinity

The increasing presence of indigenous people in public life is one of the reasons why the coherent image of *national identity* set out in *The Australian Legend* could no longer hold together, and the recognition of racial difference has also contributed to an understanding that unitary notions of *masculinity* are no longer viable.

In Charles Chauvel's classic film, *Jedda* (1955), the first Australian film to be shot in colour, Aboriginality is presented as profoundly 'other' to Anglo identity. The film is, of course, shot through with racist discourses, but because of the importance of indigenous people to the narrative Chauvel does not just represent this racial difference as something to define Anglo identity against. Instead there is a prominent and striking representation of Aboriginal masculinity in the figure of Marbuk. In some ways it may be a stereotypical image—'the primitive'—at one point he kills a crocodile with a stone knife, appearing as a kind of stone age Tarzan. But, as Colin Johnson has pointed out, Marbuk 'is allowed to dominate the film and the landscape'.[19] Johnson has offered an Aboriginal reading of the film, noting, among other things, the attraction of Marbuk, for 'Mission-educated Aboriginal women when confronted by their Aboriginality in the form of an Aboriginal male...in full control of his being';[20] in the film they appear breathless with desire.

But for non-Aboriginal audiences *Jedda* must also have been centrally about the deeply threatening attraction of black masculinity. Throughout, the camera gazes longingly at the body of Marbuk, and he is presented as powerful and frightening—spiritual, desirable, exotic, and erotic. The second element of his name, 'buk', must have had resonances with the common representation of black African-American masculinity as sexual threat, and object of desire. The station owner makes a particular point of saying that he wants Marbuk to camp well away from the family.

Threatening but attractive. Indigenous masculinity in *Jedda*, 1955

In the late 1970s, the much more politically sensitive *Chant of Jimmy Blacksmith* is an attempt to demonstrate the problems facing indigenous people, and it explicitly acknowledges that they are defined outside the traditional versions of Australian identity, and that this should not be so. But *The Chant of Jimmy Blacksmith* too, raises the fear and attraction of Aboriginal masculinity for non-indigenous audiences, opening with Jimmy living with an Anglo woman. Johnson is probably correct when he argues that, in spite of its attempts at sensitivity, 'the image lingering on is that of a berserk boong hacking to death white ladies'.[21] In the course of the film black masculinity as sexual threat is displaced into black masculinity as violent threat.

In the early nineties, Dougie Dooligan, the male lead in *Blackfellas* is gazed at longingly by the camera, as was Marbuk in *Jedda*. But Dougie is carefully not depicted as sexually threatening; in fact there is a kind of running joke about whether his motor has stalled, as Polly puts it. *Blackfellas* offers two distinct models of masculinity for those excluded from mainstream male power by their Aboriginality. Pretty Boy Floyd embodies a model of what is often known as protest masculinity. The features of his lifestyle—the drinking, the sexual activity, the shoplifting, the petty theft, and the joy-riding—can be seen as markers of deliberate resistance to dominant Anglo culture. Pretty Boy lives out what John Fiske would call 'a life of freedom, of the here and now, that radically opposes ... school, the family, marriage or work, with their emphasis on the future, on responsibility and conforming to the social norms'.[22] The behaviour of Pretty Boy deliberately opposes dominant notions of what is proper, and even dominant notions of 'private property', although it is a resistance without concrete political effects.

Dougie Dooligan, on the other hand, wishes to escape the Pretty Boy lifestyle by establishing a horse stud on Yitticup, country which has been of spiritual significance to his ancestors. The Yitticup option is proposed as a way of retaining links with Aboriginal values, while living in harmony with dominant non-indigenous culture. Dougie is not setting out to make a profit from Yitticup, just to have a sustainable, organic life there, connected with the land. There are problems with what *Blackfellas* proposes—Yitticup is gained through an individualist and competitive masculinity, a western model; and there is no space for a positive urban Aboriginality. But the film does at least acknowledge different forms of proud Aboriginal masculinity.

### New directions/new possibilities
In 1992, after a period without major successes, the industry felt re-invigorated by two low budget films which enjoyed significant box office returns and critical acclaim—*Strictly Ballroom* and *Romper Stomper*. Both dealt with multiculturalism in an urban setting—*Strictly Ballroom* offering a 'feel good' story of successful multiculturalism in relation to a 'safe' ethnic group, the Spanish; and *Romper Stomper* offering a more negative depiction of a response to Asian immigration. Both films also operated as responses to the gloom of the early 1990s recession, and both offer narratives about masculinity in the context of multiculturalism and recession.

If Scott Hastings is in some vague way a descendant of the wild colonial boy, rebelling against authority figures, he embodies a kind of masculinity that could hardly be further from the frontier. In fact the ballroom dancer is the kind of figure, who in many circles would be treated as an instance of what Connell calls subordinated masculinity—someone expelled from the circle of legitimacy set out by hegemonic masculinity.[23]

*Strictly Ballroom* is an example of the culture's policing of masculinity. Scott's version might be appropriate for the high camp world of ballroom dancing—in spite of the Chesty Bond singlet—but it is not adequate for him to reach an appro-

Learning 'proper' masculinity in *Strictly Ballroom*, 1990.

priate adult masculinity according to the film. *Strictly Ballroom* is initially somewhat critical of the patriarchal control which Fran's father, Rico, exerts within the
family, but the film ultimately approves of his demonstration of a masculinity
marginalised through ethnicity and class, but powerful in contexts like this. In
effect Rico's stereotypical Latin passion invigorates Scott's flaccid performance of
the *paso doble*, so that he *becomes* a kind of bullfighter—proud, forceful, dominating. So Scott learns the proper *paso doble* with its 'proper' masculinity from Rico—
with some help from the grandmother, as Kay Schaffer recently reminded me, and
in the closing segment of the film, his successful performance of dance and
gender is given centre stage.

There is also, in *Strictly Ballroom*, an equally important—and parallel—narrative
of the gradual re-masculinisation of Scott's father Doug—played by Barry Otto.
Through most of the film we see him as hopelessly ineffectual—another example
of subordinated masculinity—barely opening his mouth, unless to give himself
another spray of Cedel breath freshener. Shirley, his wife, constantly belittles him,

addressing him as 'you stupid man', and berates him for not doing anything—with some justification. But finally he stands up for himself, insisting that Scott listens to what he has to say, and then, more importantly, he defies his wife. The film finishes with Doug and Shirley dancing together—with him leading, as we are told should be the case, in ballroom dancing, and in life—so that hegemonic masculinity is restored twice over, at the film's conclusion. Evidently that's what you needed to do to have a ballroom dancer as the male lead in an Australian film in 1992.

*Romper Stomper*, showing in cinemas at the same time as *Strictly Ballroom*, is similarly an acknowledgment that traditional Anglo models of Australian identity are no longer viable, but instead of celebrating a new diversity, it depicts a skinhead subculture fighting a rear guard action in trying to cling to that old identity.

The skinheads' response to their marginalised position is to embody a protest masculinity similar to that lived out by Pretty Boy and his 'bros' in *Blackfellas*. Feelings of powerlessness can be at least partially dissipated by a focus on bodily pleasures, and also by exaggerating aspects of hegemonic masculinity, and exercising physical power over others without power—women, gays, ethnic minorities. The film may also have connections with a kind of masculinity associated with fascism, one which 'glorified' 'irrationally ... and the unrestrained violence of the frontline soldier'.[24] In spite of fears about the film's impact on impressionable audiences, the kind of excessive masculinity embodied by the skins is very effectively shown to be childish, futile and self-destructive.

Although it might not be obvious, the narrative's chief structuring element is a romance, like *Strictly Ballroom*. Hando is not a suitable romance hero, and he is replaced by Davey. As in the classic romance, the harsh hero, Davey, is softened by the influence of an independent woman. One of the chief contrasts between the two men is the sex scenes. Hando's is fascist sex. In contrast, a later sex scene with Davey in the room out the back of his grandmother's place is carefully set up to establish, among other things, gentleness, and equality in bed. Here too, the editing has been heavy, not particularly to tone the scene down, but more to show that they take turns to be on top, and that he is interested in her pleasure.

In fact *Romper Stomper* contains a narrative about masculinity similar in structure to that in *Strictly Ballroom*. Davey's association with Gabe emasculates him—he becomes 'over softened'. But in the film's final segment we see him regaining the power that is essential to traditional masculinities, and when he plunges the Hitler youth knife into the back of Hando's neck, Davey re-emerges as a fully masculinized hero, strong, but loving towards Gabe. Both films, then, depict ethnically diverse societies, but Rico, Scott and Doug Hastings, and Davey all end up sharing a very similar masculinity, one endorsed by the narratives.

For an Australian film to have a ballroom dancer as its male lead might have been a substantial departure, but that pales into insignificance in comparison with what we have in *The Adventures of Priscilla Queen of the Desert*, although the camp atmosphere of *Strictly Ballroom* and *Muriel's Wedding* was certainly a precursor to *Priscilla*. Stephen Elliott's vision of three drag queens cruising through the outback and confronting stereotypes of Australianness offers a significant step in destabilising fixed notions of what it means to be a man in Australia. After Terence Stamp's portrayal of the transsexual Bernadette; Guy Pearce as the effervescent and high camp, Felicia; Hugo Weaving as the gay drag performer, Mitzi, and father, Tick (same person, different roles); and Bill Hunter as the ocker male who falls in love with Bernadette, it is no longer easy to suggest that there is an essential masculinity, or to depict it as unitary and whole.

The three drag queens can be described as instances of what has been called 'incomplete performance. They create and expose key elements of an idealised femininity, while simultaneously destabilising the notion of a cohesive and controlling male identity behind the feminine mask'.[25] As Rose Lucas suggests, 'in its play between costumes and displays of various kinds', *Priscilla* explicitly questions

> the seemingly inherent relationship between certain kinds of anatomical bodies and gendered notions of masculinity and femininity. As bodies are surgically altered, as external apparel, face paint, voice pitch and modulation are changed, as varied sexual desires are expressed, we are asked to critique the complex terrain of masculinity, ultimately questioning the viability of any sustained category, or set of defining characteristics, about what constitutes the masculine.

*Priscilla*'s utopian vision of a tolerant and accepting society can perhaps best be seen at the conclusion of the film when Tick's son Benjamin '*wants* his father to have a boyfriend and *wants* to see him lipsync Abba.[26] The film certainly demonstrates the antagonism in the outback towards its vision of fluid gender identities, but it is highly critical of that antagonism.

One of the most important moments in *Priscilla*'s depiction of masculinity is the scene when Hugo Weaving, trying to conform to traditional Australian ways of being a man for his son's benefit, appears as a stockman. As one critic has commented, here 'he looks for the first time as if he is *really* in drag'.[27] The scene is not merely demonstrating that Tick cannot manage to conform to that model of frontier masculinity, it is suggesting that the Akubra, the boots, the moleskins, the tinnie are, like other signifiers of masculinity, costumes to be put on—only one of many possible costumes for men to wear.

On the other hand, there are several reasons why the euphoria which this film has sometimes elicited needs to be tempered. Although it might be currently unfashionable to say this in the wake of the influence of Judith Butler, it is *also* true that drag can be a parody of femininity, and that it can sometimes be, at least in part, the product of misogyny. Whether or not that is the case here, the film *does* reveal a deep misogyny in other ways, and, at times, a deep racism. Robertson has pointed out that in *Priscilla* it is not all identities which are represented as 'potentially fluid and mobile... the film insists on the authenticity and fixity of others in the film',[28] particularly the identity of 'woman' and 'immigrant'.

*Priscilla* betrays its misogyny—and positions its audience to share that misogyny —in a couple of scenes set in that temple of archetypal Australian masculinity, the pub. The first of these is when a woman antagonistic to the trio is 'put in her place' with a 'joke' about an exploding tampon; the second is in the scene where the audience is positioned to share the drag queens' disgust at Sylvia, the Filipina, shooting ping pong balls from her vagina while standing on the bar.

Bill Hunter's role is relevant here. In *Strictly Ballroom* and *Muriel's Wedding* he has played essentially the same character—a version of hegemonic masculinity— and both of those films have been merciless critiques of the brutal and manipulative control he exerts on a ballroom dance federation and a nuclear family, respectively. After some initial doubts on the audience's part, in *Priscilla* he is valorised as a gentle ocker bloke who falls in love with a transsexual. In fact, though, from Cynthia, his Filipina wife's point of view, he would be the same patriarchal and imprisoning character as he was in the two earlier films, literally locking her up in her house, so that she cannot perform her gendered identity in the way she wishes. But that is not the viewpoint the audience is pushed towards.

And there are similar problems with *The Sum of Us*. Again, it is impressive in its openness about homosexuality, and utopian in its depiction of Jack Thompson as the ocker bloke and loving father who is proud of his rugby-playing and gay son. But this film, too, exhibits a certain misogyny. The narrative has the Jack Thompson character being given a massive stroke by the repressed woman he wants to marry, and it finishes with her being rejected in favour of a cosy, ocker, all-male world where the son and his boyfriend look after the paralysed father. If ever there was a film about getting the mating back into mateship, *The Sum of Us* was it.

Films like *Priscilla* and *The Sum of Us* may not ultimately provide images of a non-hierarchical masculinity, defining their positive representations of non-dominant masculinities against female or racial 'others' as they do, but they certainly contribute to the diversity of images available in our cultural imaginary. So, too, do the representations in many other films, such as the gentler versions of masculinity one finds in Paul Cox films, or the sensitive new-age guy played by Matt Day in *Love and Other Catastrophes* and, at least initially, in *Doing Time for Patsy Cline*, or the similarly sensitive young musician in *All Men Are Liars*. And, of course, much more radical things are going on in experimental film and short film. Alongside these, are a diverse range of other complex representations, such as the brutalised and brutalising father in *Shine*, or the gentle and loving father in *The Castle* or *Blackrock* and *Idiot Box*'s explorations of protest masculinity.

Today, particular masculinities are deeply implicated in the organized violence of warfare, in technologies and economic behaviour that is destroying the environment, and in domestic violence, and barriers to women's equality.[29] But men are also working to forge non-hierarchical masculinities—masculinities not predicated on some form of dominance. The filmic influences on boys growing up in Australia are, of course, chiefly from global culture, not from Australian culture. But they grow up to be men in Australia, and Australian films are an important site for the examination of the problems and possibilities for masculinity in this country.

### Acknowledgments

Australian Film Finance Corporation; Polygram Filmed Entertainment; NSW Film and Television Office and Latent Image Productions for the image from *The Adventures of Priscilla, Queen of the Desert*, (Used on the cover of this book); H.C. McIntyre Trust and Susanne Carlsson for the image from *Jedda*; M & A Film Corporation for the image from *Strictly Ballroom*.

### Notes

1    Brian McFarlane, *Australian Cinema 1970-1985* (William Heinemann: Richmond, 1987)

2    Ina Bertrand & William D Routt, 'The Big Bad Combine: Some Aspects of National Aspirations and International Constraints in the Australian Cinema, 1896-1929', in *The Australian Screen* (ed. Albert Moran and Tom O'Regan, Penguin: Ringwood, 1989) pp.3-27

3    Neil Rattigan, *Images of Australia. 100 Films of the New Australian Cinema* (Southern Methodist University Press: Dallas, 1991)

4    R.W. Connell, *Masculinities* (Allen & Unwin: St Leonards, 1995)

5    ibid. p214

6    Marilyn Lake, 'The politics of respectability: Identifying the masculinist context' in Susan Magarey, Sue Rowley and Susan Sheridan (eds.) *Debutante nation: Feminism contests the 1890s* (Allen & Unwin: Sydney, 1993)

7    Graeme Turner, *Film as Social Practice* (Routledge: London & New York, 1993)

8    Allan Thomas, 'Camping Outback: Landscape, Masculinity, and Performance in The Adventures of Priscilla, Queen of the Desert', *Continuum* Vol. 10, no. 2 (1996) pp. 97-110

9    ibid. p. 101

10   Meaghan Morris, 'Personal Relationships and Sexuality', in *The New Australian Cinema* (ed. Scott Murray, Nelson/Cinema papers: Melbourne, 1980)

11   ibid. p147

12   Rose Lucas, 'Dragging It Out: Tales of Masculinity in Australian Cinema', *Meridian* Vol. 15, no. 2 (1996) pp. 207-219

13   ibid. p215

14   Thomas, 'Camping Outback: Landscape, Masculinity, and Performance in *The Adventures of Priscilla, Queen of the Desert*', pp. 97-110

15   Lucas 'Dragging It Out: Tales of Masculinity in Australian Cinema', p. 103

16   ibid. p. 212

17   Tom O'Reagan, 'Fair Dinkum Fillums: The Crocodile Dundee Phenomenon', in *The Imaginary Industry*, ed. Susan Dermody and Elizabeth Jacka, (Australian Film Television and Radio: Sydney, 1988) pp. 155-75

18  Tom O'Reagan, 'Cinema Oz: The Ocker Films', in *The Australian Screen*, ed. Albert Moran and Tom O'Regan (Penguin: Ringwood: Victoria, 1989) pp. 75-98

19  Colin Johson, 'Chauvel and the Centring of the Aboriginal Male in Australian Film', *Continuum* 1 (1987) pp. 47-56

20  ibid. p. 48

21  ibid. p. 50

22  John Fiske, Bob Hodge & Graeme Turner, *Myths of Oz: Reading Australian Popular Culture* (Allen & Unwin: Sydney, 1987)

23  Connell *Masculinities*, p. 79

24  ibid. p. 193

25  Rachel Fensham, 'Transvestophilia and Zgynemimesis: Performative Strategies and Feminist Theory', *Cultural Studies* Vol. 10, no. 3 (1996) pp. 483-97

26  Pamela Robertson, 'The Adventures of Priscilla in Oz', *Media International Australia* No. 78 (November 1995) pp. 33-38

27  Fensham 'Transvestophilia and Zgynemimesis: Performative Strategies and Feminist Theory', p. 492

28  Robertson 'The Adventures of Priscilla in Oz', p. 34

22  Connell, *Masculinities*.

*Andrew Watson*

# Australia and China— What Next?

The topic of this article is, I think, one of the most crucial foreign affairs issues facing Australia as we approach the end of this century, and that is what is happening in China and what does it mean for Australia?

It is highly likely that over the next twenty five years China will emerge as the largest economy in the world. Even if in *per capita* terms it is still not the richest per person, its economic strength will be immense, and alongside that, it will become one of the strategically most important countries in the world and in our region. It is already a major power in the Asian region and one to which we have to pay great attention. Our economic and political relationship with China will have a central impact on how our future economic and strategic position develops in the world and in the Asian region.

Yet having said that, we still face many questions over the nature of the Chinese political system. Will the Chinese political system be able to reform alongside the process of economic reform? Can we expect economic reform to lead China to become a more democratic or a more open society? In what way will China use its economic strength? Is there a possibility that China could become a threat to the region, or a problem for us?

Since 1997 was the twenty-fifth anniversary of the establishment of diplomatic relations between Australia and China, it seems to me that it is a good moment to take stock of where we have been and what issues face us. Yet the more I think

Andrew Watson is Professor of Asian Studies, co-Director of the Chinese Economy Research Unit, and Associate Dean (Research) in the Division of Humanities and Social Sciences, University of Adelaide. He is also President of the Chinese Studies Association of Australia, a member of the Board of the Australia China Council, and from 1993 to 1996 he was a member of the Australian Research Council's Asian and Social Sciences Panel. He is the author of, among other things: *Living in China* (Batsford) 1975; the translator of *Mao Zedung: Economic and Financial Problems* (Cambridge University Press) 1980; and editor of *Economic Reform and Social Change in China* (Routledge) 1992.

about the issues, the more complex they become, and some of the potential problems need careful thought.

In July 1997 at the Chinese Studies Association of Australia Conference which was held in Adelaide a very senior visitor from China, Mr Zhu Qizhen gave a speech which represented the Chinese government's view of how the relationship between Australia and China was in the twenty-fifth anniversary year. Mr Zhu is Vice Chairman of the Foreign Affairs Committee of the National People's Congress. He was one of the first Chinese diplomats to come to Australia in 1973 and he was also deputy Minister of Foreign Affairs for many years. So he spoke with a very long knowledge of Australia, and in fact with many friends in Australia. His overall assessment was very positive. He stressed what he saw as successful co-operation between Australia and China in the Asia Pacific region. He felt that working together the two countries had successfully managed to solve or deal with important issues in the region. He also stressed the very strong economic complementarities between the two countries and on that basis he was very optimistic about the future. He did, however, make a fairly clear statement of principle. He said:

> Since taking office the Coalition government of Australia has on many occasions stated its position on the One China Policy and to recognise Tibet as part of Chinese territory. A number of leaders of your government have also reiterated this position of the government's on various occasions. We appreciate all this. However, it should be pointed out that the questions of Taiwan and Tibet involving China's state sovereignty and territorial integrity have always been sensitive political issues on which the smooth development of our bilateral relationship hinges. These issues if not handled properly will damage our bilateral relations or even lead to their retrogression.[1]

In other words, it seems to me Mr Zhu gave us a fairly clear statement of what issues China sees as very sensitive and which could cause difficulty in the relationship between us.

In her response to that speech Penny Wensley—who was then Acting Deputy Secretary of the Department of Foreign Affairs and Trade, and has since become our Ambassador to the United Nations—did not directly address those two points. Instead, she stressed that Australia places great importance on a human rights dialogue with China, and she argued that the relationship should be mature enough for difficult issues to be handled in an open and understanding way. In that context she looked forward to the visit by an Australian human rights delegation to China, a visit which took place in the middle of August 1997.[2]

Both sides at the conference signalled what they thought were the most sensitive issues in the relationship, the issues which are most likely to become a challenge, or could be, if not handled properly. Nevertheless, against that background they both took a very positive view of the current state of affairs of the immediate prospects.

Listening to them speak, I was struck by how different the picture was just one year earlier. The Australian press was full of stories of the China threat and asking what was China doing in the South China Seas. The relationship with Taiwan was shaped by the aftermath of the Taiwan elections and the Chinese military tests in the area. Meanwhile the new Coalition government in Australia was renewing a defence interaction with the United States (US) in ways which made some commentators in the Chinese press describe us and Japan as the crab's claws directed at China. So, clearly, in the second half of 1996 the relationship between Australia and China was very uncertain, and Australia's view that the relationship was robust enough to be able to discuss sensitive issues without affecting stability was under threat. There was a potential for crisis. And yet one year later the two countries were once again enjoying a positive interaction. So it seems appropriate to reflect on the nature of this relationship.

I will do this by addressing three issues. First I want to consider the underlying logic of the Australia/China relationship: it seems to me that while that relationship is clearly and firmly rooted in economic and trade issues, there are also very important political and strategic interactions. Secondly, I will trace the ways in which the relationship has evolved, and focus particularly on 1996 and 1997 and the sorts of difficulties that have emerged to upset what at one time seemed to be a very comfortable relationship. Finally, I will touch on some of the difficulties and some of the challenges that face us in our relationship with China, particularly as we move into the next century. It seems to me that there are some sensitive issues for us to consider when we interact with China, which will need careful handling.

First of all, the underlying logic. China, of course, is now one of Australia's big markets. It has consistently been in the top five or six of our trading partners for a good number of years, and as its economy grows it will continue to increase in importance. Figure 1 illustrates the pattern of our trade with China, and it shows quite clearly the substantial surge that has occurred in the 1990s. After a long period of relatively slow but steady growth, in the past few years trade with China has been growing at something like twenty percent a year. This has happened at the same time as the growth of trade with some other parts of the world has tended to slow down. So China's role in our world trade is clearly becoming more important. It has emerged alongside the other Asian trading nations as a major partner. In fact in 1996 it was our fifth largest market. Japan was still well out in front, but China was alongside South Korea, Taiwan and Hong Kong. Now that Hong Kong is part of China, if we combine the Hong Kong and China total, then the Chinese world is second most important. Until the Asian Economic Crisis, the prospects were for continued strong growth. Much now depends on whether China can weather the impact. If so, its trade relationship will be even further enhanced. The way China manages the aftermath of the crisis will also be crucial for both the region and for Australia. A successful outcome will make things much easier.

A$ millions

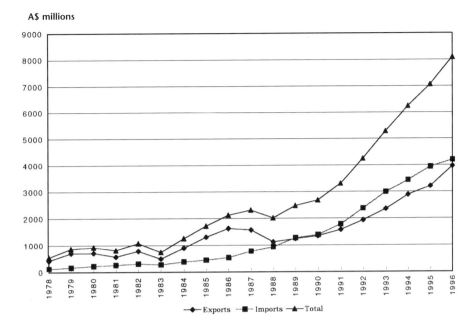

Figure 1. Australian trade with China, 1978–96

On the other hand, if China is also severely affected—and it is already experiencing declines in trade and investment growth—the regional revival will be slower to achieve.

Within that trade, Australian exports are mainly primary products. We export a lot of wool, wheat, barley, iron ore and metals, and this accounts for nearly three quarters of our trade with China. For some commodities China is very important, particularly wool, and increasingly so for iron ore and barley. There are a growing number of manufactures in our exports, and I think from Australia's point of view this is important. We need to diversify. We need to increase the amount of manufactures and of value-added products in our exports.

Our imports from China are largely labour intensive products, things like textiles, garments, light industrial products. The surge of imports from China are among one of the reasons why our own clothing industry is finding the competition difficult.

Alongside such trade, the recent opening of China's services sector to the world has seen a growth in banking, insurance and legal services moving into China. As China tries to reform its system in order to join the World Trade Organisation, opportunities for Australia in those sectors will tend to increase. So our interaction with China will tend to diversify. Alongside that development, there is growing investment, and cross-investment. Australian investment in China is not large, but in recent years it has grown quite quickly. Chinese investment in Australia is its second largest block of foreign investment after Hong Kong. It has large amounts of investment in iron ore, in farms and in meat processing in Australia.

So the economic logic is very clear, and the economic promise is very strong. But I think that within these parameters, it is important for us to understand that China is more significant for us than perhaps we are for it. For us China is something like five percent of our international trade. We are less than two per-cent of China's trade with the rest of the world, so the economic dimension of this relationship is more significant for us.

Alongside that economic story, however, there are also very many significant regional and strategic considerations. For example, China plays a central role in dealing with a number of important issues including North Korea, Cambodia, the South China Seas. From Australia's point of view, therefore, it is very important to keep China engaged in discussion and in strategic interaction to try to handle these issues. It is very important for Australia to try to keep China engaged in regional processes such as the Asian-Pacific Economic Corporation (APEC) in order to maintain a role for China in handling those problems. In this respect, Australia's position is somewhat different from that of other countries. The US, for example, would view China in a rather different way. The US would be less reliant on China and it would be more concerned to see China as a potential challenge to its dominant position in the world. For us, having a positive and stable relationship with China is far more important. So the logic of our engagement with China, rests on very obvious economic and strategic considerations.

This now brings me to my second topic which is how has the relationship evolved and what is the basis of Australia's approach? Until the late 1960s Australia's perceptions of China were dominated by fear. It was expressed in the title of Gregory Clarke's 1967 book *In Fear of China,* and it was not until the late 1960s that this began to change. In 1972 the Whitlam government's very rapid recognition of China marked a decisive shift in Australia's relations. Since that time there has been, more or less continuously, a consensus within Australia of the importance of building a positive and stable relationship with China. By the early 1980s, this consensus had crystallised around a number of key ideas and they were recently summarised in an essay by Stuart Harris who was a former secretary of the Department of Foreign Affairs. He summed these up as essentially five principles:

1. A relationship based on friendship not fear
2. An independent Australian position
3. A sense of economic opportunities
4. The inevitability of China's emergence as a major power
5. A role in helping China engage with the world.[3]

The first was an argument that the relationship with China should be based on friendship and not fear. In other words, the way to deal with China, the way to handle the relationship, was to try to develop a positive understanding of China.

To look at China's character, its traditions and its development, and to analyse what China was doing in terms of a positive attempt to understand it, rather than an attempt to contain or reject it. Secondly, there was a need to develop an independent Australian position in relationship with China. It was important for Australia to try to distinguish its role in the Asian region separately from those of other western powers. Australia has some special characteristics in its relationship with China, and this should be reflected in its policy. Australia should not be seen as the representative of other western powers. The third feature was a very bread-and-butter one, and that is the view that economic reform and rapid economic growth offered a range of new opportunities for Australia. The potential was there for China to take over something of the role that Japan once had in pushing our economy forward, and therefore it was very important for Australia to engage with China, to try and help China's reforms progress, and through those reforms to help realise the opportunities that would arise. The fourth principle was a recognition that China was inevitably going to become a major regional and world power. Australian policy had to be shaped to reflect that fact. Finally therefore, Australia's security depended on engaging with China, on helping China to join the world on an equal basis and not as trying to contain China or trying to limit its impact.

Despite the many changes that have taken place since the early 1980s, it seems to me that these principles still remain central to Australia's diplomatic approach to China.

In political terms, the high point of our relationship came between 1983 and 1988. Political relations at that time were of course very warm. There was a constant stream of exchanges at the highest level. Prime Minister Bob Hawke developed very close friendships with some of the leading reformers in the Chinese government. Whereas the Whitlam government played ping pong with China, the Hawke government played tennis, and Bob Hawke often played with counterparts in Beijing. At the same time Australia developed a strategy which was known as the 'China Action Plan', which was formulated in 1983/84. This set out a range of strategic trade and economic targets, and there was a co-ordinated effort among government departments to try and achieve them. In practice, most of them were very quickly realised. Our trade with China doubled well before the target date. At that time, therefore, the relationship with China seemed to be very special. Many people in Australia assumed that Australia somehow had a rather unique role in what was happening in China, that we could mediate between China and the world, that we could play a role in promoting China's economic reform. It was a very positive picture of China and the future.

Not surprisingly therefore, the reaction in Australia to the savage repression of the students at Tiananmen in June 1989 and the very public way in which it was done was quite profound. I think many Australians at all levels felt betrayed by what was happening in China. They had to recognise that the Chinese

Communist Party was determined to hold onto power by any means necessary, and that the Chinese Communist Party put the stability of its government above all else. It could not be assumed therefore that economic change would inevitably bring political change, that political liberalisation was going to be the inevitable and rapid consequence of market reforms. The cosy view of China was swept aside and was replaced by a much more sober and in some ways a more cynical view, and the so-called 'China fatigue' set in. There was a sense that Australia had put a lot of effort into China but that the gains were not obvious. The relationship had lost its special edge. Although the 1990s has seen the surge in trade, and there has been a renewal of strong interaction with China at all levels, the resulting relationship has been much more pragmatic.

That was the situation until 1995. In 1995 and 1996 some challenges to this pragmatic position began to emerge. A number of events occurred. In June 1995 President Li Denghui of Taiwan was given permission to visit the US to go back to his old university. The Chinese were extremely angry. They took this as inter-ference in China's internal affairs. At the time the US Congress as a whole was tak-ing a harder stand on China on a whole range of human rights and international relations issues. The Taiwan situation became more sensitive, and at the same time the Taiwanese were beginning to push themselves for much greater recognition, for a much stronger position in the world at large. Taiwan was undertaking what was known as 'vacation diplomacy'. Its leaders would travel to countries around the world on informal visits even though it did not have recognition, and through that process the Taiwanese profile would become higher.

When the Taiwan tensions increased again as a result of the presidential elections in March 1996, and the US Navy became involved, Australia's call for moderation—for moderation on all sides—was rebuked by China as interference in Chinese affairs. It became very obvious that the Taiwan issue was not one which could be conveniently ignored and there was a potential for it to challenge the pragmatic set of principles we had developed in our relationship with China.

A second feature over the period 1995 to 1996 was the growth of perceptions of a 'China threat'. This was linked both to China's increasing economic strength and to its efforts at military modernisation, and the view was intensified by the flare-up of tensions and disputes in the South China Seas during 1995. The Philippines, Indonesia, and Vietnam all challenged China's long-standing claim to sovereignty over huge areas of the South China Seas. China responded by sending ships and troops to occupy sensitive islands. At the same time the US and Japan became very much concerned about the Sea Lanes of Communication, particular-ly because a lot of Japan's energy supply comes through this area. Questions were raised about China's aims, and the view began to grow in some countries that China was not a *status quo* power, but was a power which was potentially likely to threaten regional stability.

From Australia's point of view, the military aspects of this discussion were also heightened by China's nuclear test in 1995. We had just been rather irate at the French letting off bombs in the South Pacific, and suddenly there was China letting off bombs in Central Asia. This not only provoked a more critical public view of what China was doing, but also eventually led Australia to make some protest.

During 1996, therefore, it began to seem as if Australia might have to make some hard choices about its regional goals. It might have to begin to handle a real crisis in its relationship with China. What is more, the election of the new government, which was anxious to distinguish itself from its predecessor, reinforced this perception. Then Australia cancelled the export-subsidy scheme, reaffirmed its defence ties with the US, and the Minister of Defence, Ian MacLachlan, made a speech which seemed to endorse the view that maybe China was going to be a military threat in the region. All of these issues made the Chinese very suspicious about the direction Australia was taking, and there were real concerns as to what was happening in our relationship.

It was not until Prime Minister John Howard went to China in March 1997 that a major effort was made to turn this around. In fact when John Howard went to China, he forcefully restated Australia's position, in what was a reiteration of the five principles that had emerged during the 1980s. He focussed very much on economic issues and on a pragmatic putting-aside of hard questions which, he argued, should be handled through friendly dialogue. He stressed that Australia was independent and that its defence ties with the US did not necessarily mean that we represented the US. He also stressed a strong continuity with the previous government's position. In effect he was able to restore the emphases of the pre-1989 policies, and the efforts Australia had made at that time may well have had a lasting legacy.

When this was accompanied by Australia's rejection of a United Nations motion critical of China's human rights record, and by a very positive acceptance of the new provisional legislature in Hong Kong, the situation changed quite dramatically. Subsequently there was a rapid succession of high level exchanges. Members of the Political Bureau came to Australia, ministers went to China, and then of course in April 1997 Zhu Rongji, who is now the new premier to replace Li Peng, also came to Australia. There was thus a rapid succession of high level visits, and there was a re-establishment of the various joint economic committees that had worked so effectively in previous periods to promote strategic goals. As well, there was a revival of a human rights dialogue, and China accepted another delegation from Australia to go and discuss the issue.

In essence, therefore, it seems to me that at present the basis of the relationship has returned to those principles established in the 1980s. The prospects for further economic growth and for further diplomatic and cultural and other types of interaction look good.

So this now brings me to my final topic, which is to look at some of the issues which are lurking in the background which could potentially upset this basic situation. As 1995/96 showed, the position can easily be threatened. Those issues are of course the issues listed by Zhu Qizhen and Penny Wensley which I quoted earlier; they are issues to do with Taiwan and Tibet and human rights.

In some ways the Taiwan issue is both a straightforward one and a very complex one. On the one hand the problem is a simple one. It is something to be sorted out between Taipei and Beijing. What is the point of anybody getting in the way—you will only get hurt. On the other hand the relationship is also a very complex one. We have strong trade links and other links with Taiwan. We have lots of students from Taiwan. We have lots of cultural interaction. We exchange theatre. We exchange arts shows. We even have a *de facto* Taiwanese embassy in Canberra, the Taipei Economic and Cultural Office.

At the same time, Taiwan has increasingly strong interaction with China. Whenever I go to China I continually meet people from Taiwan who are on tours, who are visiting relatives, and who are conducting business. Taiwan has very large trade interaction with China, often via Hong Kong. Taiwan has large investments in China. In fact some analysts argue that you have to look at the Taiwan, Hong Kong, and South China coast economy as an increasingly integrated unit. Taiwan probably has something like thirty billion dollars of investment in China. So from our point of view, our optimum strategy is to sustain a pragmatic relationship and to wait for the Chinese to sort it out themselves. But on the other hand we cannot assume that all will remain quiet. That Taiwan will not say anything just to keep Australia comfortable. It is not a problem we can ignore, and it is not a problem we can actually do much about in a pro-active sense. If pressures from the US or pressures from Taiwan increase or if China responds in a particular way potential crises are there.

There is no easy answer to this one. Quite clearly a lot of Australian diplomacy is directed at trying to persuade the US to adopt a more cautious policy, at trying to encourage the Taiwanese not to push too hard, at trying to find ways to allow the internationalisation of the Chinese economy to help solve the problem itself. Australia's position, like that of the US, is that there is only one China and its government is in Beijing. Conflict, however would create many intense problems for Australia to deal with.

The other two issues of Tibet and human rights of course are very closely linked. Both are likely to remain very sensitive issues for a long time, and even if the government might like them to go away, the Australian media and social pressure within Australia are likely to keep the issues alive. There are always going to be aspects where people are going to challenge China's record. I suppose the question is whether attacking China forcefully on these issues and demanding change is likely to be the most effective way of producing it. In some ways I find it ironic that currently in China we have a reformist government which has done more than most governments in most periods since 1949 to improve basic rights, and yet it finds itself inevitably the subject of very strong criticism. Clearly, China is still paying a heavy price for Tiananmen. There are limits to civil and political freedoms in China and the dominance of the state is still not curbed by the rule of law.

To date the official Australian position has been that the best way to approach these issues is one of dialogue and interaction, rather than confrontation. Those are essentially the sorts of policies that have been developed during the 1980s and the early 1990s. They were the policies of the previous government and they are by and large being maintained by the current one. The set of policies on this issue have five main elements.[4]

First of all is the view that human rights are a rather complex mix. That they combine economic and social and cultural and other rights alongside civil and political ones, and that we need to take a whole picture into account when we make some analysis of human rights. Secondly, from that it follows that efforts to improve human rights or to affect human rights in other countries, can be broken down into a number of separate and practical areas. You can talk about labour rights or labour laws, criminal laws, treatment of criminals, administrative codes, constitutional laws and so on, and it is quite often possible to develop co-operative work in these areas and thereby to contribute to the overall dialogue on human rights. The third aspect therefore is that efforts to improve human rights must be based on dialogue and on efforts to understand each other's cultural and social context. You need to be able to sustain a dialogue if you are going to be able to do anything about them. The fourth issue is that talking about human rights to others also means being prepared to recognise your own problems in this area. Lastly, there should be consistency across the issue for all nations. It is not appropriate to treat China in one way and to treat another country in another way. If you are going to deal with this issue you deal with it as consistently as you can. In that respect, it is interesting to note that Foreign Affairs Minister Alexander Downer would not sign a treaty with the European Union because it was one in which Europe tried to link the economic issues directly with human rights issues in Australia.

Quite clearly this set of ideas is very practical. On the other hand, it has provided a basis for talking to China. In 1991 Australia was the first country to send an international delegation to China to discuss human rights. The second Australian delegation went in 1993 and the third delegation went in August 1997. Now many might say, 'Well, it's hard to see that these exchanges have had any practical outcomes. They've simply allowed some parliamentarians and others to go to China and to ask some questions about what's being done'. But it seems to me that they do consistently send the signal to China that this is an important issue. That it will remain on the agenda.

In my view, as China becomes richer and as it interacts more and more with the world, it will remain vital to sustain that dialogue. We have to keep China aware of our concerns, just as China makes its concerns clear to us.

To try and work through those issues sometimes requires a pragmatic approach. And that Australia's efforts over many years to build a positive relationship with China provides a good basis for such interaction.

In conclusion, therefore, it would seem that keeping engaged with China, helping its reform process and meanwhile maintaining a dialogue on difficult issues is the best option. It is not possible to shut China out. It is too large a country, and it is too central to many key issues in the region.

### Notes

1   Keynote speech by Mr Zhu Qizhen at the conference marking the 25th anniversary of the establishment of diplomatic relations between China and Australia, Fifth Chinese Studies Association of Australia, University of Adelaide, 16 July 1997

2   Penny Wensley, 'Australia-China Relations Review and Prospects for the next 25 years', Keynote speaker at the conference.

3   Stuart Harris, 'Australia-China, Political relations, 1985-95: Fear, Friendly Relations or What?' in Colin MacKerras (ed.), *Australia and China: Partners in Asia* (Macmillan: Australia, 1996) pp. 7-21.

4   The following discussion draws on Ann Kent, 'Human Rights in Australia-China Relations, 1985-95', in Mackerras (ed.), *Australia and China: Partners in Asia.*